cricket with balls

the year of the balls

2008: a disrespective

Written by Jrod (Jarrod Kimber)

Guest writer Miriam Laila Ahamat

First Published 2009

Published by Lulu

Index

Foreword – page 5

Introduction – page 9

2007 – page 11

January - page 13

February - page 32

March – page 47

April – page 58

May – page 66

June – page 81

July – page 92

August – page 105

September - page 111

October – page 118

November – page 125

December – page 146

Special Free No Questions Asked Bonus Post – page 157

Edited by Miriam Laila Ahamat & Astrid Lee

© Jarrod Kimber 2008. All rights reserved.

Cover Design by Jeremy Theobald

The Angry Cricket by Blair Kimber

CWB's prototype cricketer by Dibyo

The authors assert the moral right to be recognised as the authors.

ISBN: 978-1-4092-8239-6

For Elsie, Ken & Bonga Bonga

Without you there would be nothing here.

2008 was one of those cricket years destined for a future of totemic significance. Think 1981 (Botham). Think 1932-3 (Bodyline). Think 1978 (Craig Serjeant's only Test hundred). It was an annus mirabilis for Twenty20, an annus horribilis for the hitherto all-conquering Australian team, and a dirty, great, gaping, hairy annus for Cricket With Balls. If you're a regular reader, welcome back. If you're new to the views of the indefatigable Jrod, Sehwagology is not the latest Hollywood cult religion mixing Christian Science with colonic irrigation, and cast from your mind that Natalie Portman appeared in *Mars Attacks!* (WTF! Everyone makes mistakes, but when does Tim Burton use up his quota?). Prepare to commune with the likes of Lord Megachief of Gold (Shivnarine Chanderpaul), Cricket's Noam Chomsky (Stephen Fleming), the Play Doh Tigers (Bangladesh) and my personal favourite The Work Experience Kid (Shoaib Malik); even to savour the X-rated exploits of Jacques Kallis, Daniel Vettori and Michael Hussey.

Cricket used to be a realm where the majority of readers thought that Hunter S. Thompson was an left-handed amateur batsman of the 1920s who played three games for Leicestershire before playing regularly with I Zingari, Free Foresters and the Hampshire Hogs. Jrod throws the game's windows gloriously open, revelling in the absurdity of Rikki Clarke having played for England, and wallowing in the pain of Bryce McGain having not played for Australia. He is a writer of great panache, and a man of exquisitely-honed sensibilities. Why, by the end of 2008, he had even extended the olive branch to Graeme Smith - although if Smithy wants to stay in CWB's good graces, he'd better keep his clammy, saffa hands off Natalie. Personally, I've always thought the Year in Review genre totally naff – pre-emptive treatment for Alzheimer's. But 2008 wasn't just any year, and CWB is certainly not just any cricket blog.

GIDEON HAIGH January 2009

According to Wikipedia, a blog (a contraction of the term "Web log") is a website, usually maintained by an individual, with regular entries of commentary, descriptions of events, or other material such as graphics or video. Entries are commonly displayed in reverse-chronological order. Interesting stuff I'm sure you'll agree.

But what is Cricket With Balls? Is it a heat-seeking mutated bastard that takes the piss while storming through the online cricket world like a jilted bride with a stained dress, or a cricket website?

Cricket With Balls never meant to take over the world; it just happened. The blog was originally set up as a way of communicating with friends about cricket, but it turned into its current self-justifying self-publicising self-gratifying form shortly after.

The website has turned into a cult hit for cricket fans. Players, administracrats and writers read the site, although few would admit it. Cricket With Balls struck a chord with cricket fans that were bored with the straight narrative bland coverage of cricket, and wanted a bit of spice and fantasy sex in their cricket reporting.

Cricket With Balls did this, and then some.

It's not always right, it's not fair and balanced, it's hardly disease free, it's generally not grammatically or politically correct, it's rarely serious, but it is in fact, cricket with balls.

If you have read the site, buy the book, so one day you can say to others "really, you only just found out about Cricket With Balls, I've been reading it for ages, although I think it really jumped the shark after the book came out, it's full of corporate sell-out clap trap now, but back then, oh my, cricket blogs were truly better in my day".

They were, you know.

Jrod/Jarrod

The 2007 cricket year ended with England finishing a difficult tour in Sri Lanka, which followed with Sri Lanka getting handled in Australia. South Africa won a series in Pakistan - in the days when international cricket was still played in Pakistan - then South Africa demoralised New Zealand. Yet, they still ended up one-all at home going into 2008, against the West Indies.

The last quarter of the year saw India win the ICC World Twenty20, a victory that played a significant part in the way cricket evolved in 2008. All the while Canada struggled against Kenya without John Davison.

2008 began with India about to play Australia in Sydney in the second Test of one of the most controversial series of recent times. A race row had erupted after some on-field words were exchanged between Harbhajan Singh and Andrew Symonds, and Harbhajan's position for the rest of the tour was in doubt because of possible disciplinary action. At the same time, Australia was considering whether to cancel their forthcoming tour to Pakistan. Cricket With Balls' 2008 disrespective starts with a look at Australia's attitude to touring.

Or to put it another way -

A long long time ago in a cricket season far away…

The period of 2008 would start with a continental war between Australia and India, the evil Galactic Empire was still holding on the power, but the rebel alliances had begun to strip the facade. Other nations now knew that this was not an indestructible force, and were lining up to take their chance. The Empire couldn't be taken down by one opponent, but there was more than one opponent lining up to restore freedom to the Galaxy…

January 1st - Australia's new touring guideline

This post was written because Australia hadn't toured Pakistan since 1998, which is their prerogative, but it was the way they wouldn't pull out early, and would string it out like they were really considered going that inspired this post.

In the media, Australia are talking about not touring Pakistan, but behind ivory doors they are apparently looking at changing the criteria Australia uses when touring any country. Luckily I have a mole on the inside. I just received this letter under my hotel room door, which is spooky, cause I'm not staying in a hotel.

Hi Cricket With Balls,

You may not remember me, I'm the faceless corporate cricket official, we met at a Cricket Australia event, it was the Duck and Dom Pérignon night at the Melbourne Club. I'm a big fan of your site, I find it very liberating compared to the normal staid proper cricket sites, plus I like talking about balls. Anyhoo, in the spirit of helping out all forms of media, I thought I'd give you the latest information straight from Cricket Australia's Waugh room. Cricket Australia has decided to only tour countries in the future that live up to the socio-economical and free democratic world that Australia is fighting for.

Australia's new touring guidelines

Bangladesh – We will only play them when they find bowlers capable of taking five wickets a test, and if they join the coalition of the willing.
England – No matter how many bombs blow up there or how stinky they continue to be, we shall fight them on the pitches for now and for ever, great chaps they are.
India – Happy to tour there if Navjot Sidhu is locked up, they join the coalition of the willing and when they successfully dye the colour of their skin to something more acceptable.
New Zealand – Due to recent developments, games against NZ will be downgraded to first class games, but if they continue to let refugees run free, we may play all first class games against them at home for safety reasons.
Pakistan – All tours are cancelled until they accept Jesus as their saviour, or George W Bush.
South Africa – We will continue to tour there, but we would prefer the land was given back to its rightful owners, white diamond merchants and British aristocrats.
Sri Lanka – We refuse to tour while the Sri Lankan government supports chuckers.
West Indies – Too many poor black people live there, they scare us.

Cheers and best wishes to you and all of the people you care for in the silly season,

FCCO

January 4 - Why Ponting and Kumble should be suspended

The concept of this post came as I sat in the grandstand at the G. Watching slow over rates on TV is bad, but you can do other things that pass the time. Watching it at the ground is excruciating, and it came back to bite Australia later on in the year.

Test cricket is paid for by us, the punters. Not cricket administracrats. Not Russian mafia. Not Indian television companies. Not Pepsi. By us. If we didn't love cricket, Pepsi wouldn't put money in, TV wouldn't pay for the rights, and cricket administracrats wouldn't fly around the world repeating phrases written by publicity robots. I'm not sure why I mentioned the mafia.

As a paying public, we should have a say in how the game is played, and I say it is played too fuckin' slow. I'm not talking about runs per over, I'm talking about lazy arse teams in the field. Over rates are getting worse. The ICC doesn't care, they impose no real sanctions other than taking a few stray dollars of captains once in a blue moon.

How many captains have been suspended? I can sort of remember one; Ganguly (I think), and that's it. Not good enough. The over rates at the SCG for this Test are horrible, I'm talking John Travolta in Look Who's Talking horrible. I think Ponting, Kumble and Graeme Smith should be suspended for at least two Tests each.

Ponting and Kumble for their bad over rates, Smith cause he's a shit bloke. Who is with me?

January 5 - Oh no you didn't

This was from the West Indies tour of South Africa.

From time to time, I like to call South Africans evil. I'm not sure if they are really evil, like say Republicans or reality TV producers, but they do seem to have a large proportion of people who are extremely hard to like. Actually, how about I put it this way, they are probably evil in a cricket sense, but I'm sure they donate to charity, give bibles to poor children (who hopefully burn them for warmth) or help their maids carry out the bins.

Why was I talking about this, ok got it, Cape Town, Evil Empire vs the Windies. Shivnarine "Lord Megachief" Chanderpaul (©kingcricket.co.uk) was still at the crease, he had just shared a partnership with Fidel Edwards, a man whose batting skill is questionable at best. Before today his average was below four. Ol' Shiv decides to let Fidel take the strike (seen this before), and after playing and missing by at least six inches for about 10 balls I switched over to a film, a black and white Clooney film to be exact. Seen it before, but I hate to see South Africa win.

After a few minutes I switched back, somehow, against all logic, and Fidel started to hit the ball and got himself to 20 odd. The Evil Empire were sledging him, probably a bit too much, due to his number 11 skill level. I may be Australian, and I may love sledging, but any team who abuses a number 11 for getting away a few slogs is a bit low. Unless it's Victoria; they can do no wrong.

I flicked between Senator Joe attacking Ed Murrow, and Fidel swinging away like a drunken farmer. Both were hard to watch. Eventually he fell on his shovel. This left the Windies with a nine for a 110ish lead. Even though Fidel was number 11, Chris Gayle came in next. He had retired hurt earlier in the innings. Not content with his dicky hammy, he had copped one on the glove from Andre Nel which had shattered his thumb. He said he would bat if necessary. Apparently he deemed it necessary.

South Africa did what any team full of fast bowlers would have done, they bowled short and aimed at his broken thumb. Problem is Gayle just swung away; in one over from Nel, he hit him for 16. Sometimes with just one hand on the bat. He defended a ball from the left arm oddodox Paul Harris and winced, so next ball he slogged him over mid wicket.

Gayle then smashed Dale Steyn for consecutive sixes. I mentioned he had a broken thumb, didn't I? After the two sixes, Steyn gets Gayle caught on the rope at long on for 38 off 48 balls. A 70-odd partnership with Lord Megachief. Steyn then sends Gayle off. I shit you not, he sends off a batsman who has just hit him for 12 runs in two balls with a broken thumb. And it wasn't a subtle Sreesanth send off. He turned and screamed at him, then other South Africans tried to push him off the field, and he continued to scream at him.

Gayle was Gayle, he looked pretty unfazed by it. But Steyn continued some sort of evil tirade against him. How many batsmen in world cricket would bat with a newly fractured thumb? Of the few who would, how many would hit 38 off 48 balls with at least three sixes (that I saw). The man comes from the hospital to play when his country needs him, probably against all medical advice, and then he gets some short balls and puts them in the crowd, and they abuse him. What sort of team is this?

I can understand frustration, I can understand a fast bowler getting angry, I can understand being hit for sixes (too well), but screaming at a guy who did what Gayle did is a pretty low act. Another thing to add to my Evil South Africa list, and another thing to add to my Chris Gayle is a cool mofo file. Good Night & Good Luck.

January 7 - Is Steve Symonds's daddy?

The next few posts are about the infamous Sydney test debacle. Bad umpiring, Australians cheating, Indians getting stroppy, and bastard monkeys.

Australia lead two-nil. No amount of histrionics will change that.

India can rightfully think they were hard done by. But will it change the score line? If India get too caught up in this they will lose the series four-nil. They got shafted, it has happened to all sporting teams in the world. This one was pretty full on, no doubt, but shit happens. India are the closest team on pure ability to Australia, but if they think they lost just because of umpiring decisions they would be making a huge mistake.

Blaming the umpires sells a lot of papers, but it doesn't win you the next Test, and that is all India can do. You don't win respect in the media, you win it on the turf. India should look at this game critically, because they made mistakes, mistakes you can't afford against Australia. Andrew Symonds should have been given out, but India's mistake was letting a batsman of Brad Hogg's ability take the momentum away from them. They bowled horribly to him, and he turned around the innings.

In their innings Sachin Tendulkar played brilliantly, but his work with the tailenders was defensive and looked selfish. I'm not saying it was selfish, but when you are that on top of a team as India was, your champion batsman not out, and batting with below par batsmen, surely he should take over and guide the game, not let the tailenders flow along until they inevitably go out.

India's bowling in the second innings, Harbhajan's aside, wasn't of a great standard. Anil was horrible, worse than I have ever seen him before. But now they know they can make Australia bleed. Mind you a wounded beast gets even angrier. Now the test is over, Steve Bucknor's umpiring career is also over. His umpiring is about five years past its use by date. At his prime he was a damn good umpire, but Elvis got fat and Steve got deaf and blind. These things happen.

January 7 - Anil's comments

Anil's comments seemed odd to me. But if the game was a draw and Harbhajan Singh and Andrew Symonds weren't at war, we probably would have forgotten them already. Some of his appeals off his own bowling were horrible, in this very match. He appeals for LBs that wouldn't hit over-sized novelty stumps. What bowler doesn't?

His team-mate Sehwag was once suspended for excessive appealing, possibly the worst decision I can remember. A bowler or fielder's job is to appeal when they think there is a chance of a wicket. And so they should, 'cause their job as bowlers or fielders is to ask the umpire if the batsman is out. You hear a noise, you appeal, you hit a pad, and you appeal. You're at square leg and your bowler hits the pads, everyone appeals, you join in.

No bowler only appeals for balls he knows are out. Sometimes we appeal for balls we know aren't out, just to put pressure on the batsmen, sometimes we do it to work on the umpire for the one that is out. It's not in the spirit of the game, but all nationalities of cricketers do this. Australia put a lot of pressure on the umpires yesterday, no more than I have seen in Lahore or Mumbai.

Michael Clarke didn't walk when he got caught at slip. Probably 'cause Australians don't walk. I saw a guy get bowled one day and stood his ground.

Batsmen's job, batting. Bowler's job, bowling. Umpire's job, umpiring.

Harbhajan did something that Symonds didn't like, and something followed, of which I am sure Symonds will spin and Harbhajan will spin. So far Harbhajan hasn't spun it well.

While all this has gone on, South Africa had a batsman use a runner, even though they were planning on making him bowl the same day. He did bowl, he bowled quite a few overs. How can you be fit enough to bowl, but not run? Some people will call that cheating, others weak officiating, I call it the way South Africa play their cricket. Arjuna used to call for a runner because he was fat. There isn't a Test team that hasn't tested the rules. I hear a lot about the spirit of the game, I'm not even sure what it means anymore.

I do know this; bowlers and fielders have always appealed for balls they are not sure about. Australians generally don't walk. And cricketers have disagreements on the field. These days if you're Indian or Australian and you fart it makes international headlines.

Anil is a legend of cricket, but there is no doubt he goes about his cricket in a different way to Australia. He is a very intelligent guy, so why would he go into honesty pacts with Australians? I wouldn't trust my mum in backyard cricket, especially with catches.

My problem is with the hypocritical nature of Australians wanting people to trust us on certain things and not on others. But that's my next post.

January 7 - Every Aussie is an arsehole, especially me

We are.

We're not fucking arseholes, mind you, but we are arseholes.

Australia has one culture: winning. Be it Grammys, Oscars or World Cups, we do it at an amazingly high level. If we aren't the best sporting nation on earth, we are pretty damn close. There aren't many sports we don't have world-class performers in. Hell we even win winter Olympic medals. Sport is not our religion, winning is. And we are ruthless about it.

Friendships are lost. Injuries are ignored. Rules are bent. The opposition is intimidated. Anything we can do to beat you. It was the way I was brought up. On the field we believe all's fair in love and war. Sure we have moments where we are nice, even in sports, but we still want to win. Afterwards, have a beer with the guy you called a flaming arse muncher, just trying to fire you up mate, want a cold one?

Now they are dobbing in cricketers; are they serious? Either play like the arseholes we were born to be, or straighten up and fly right. Don't put your feet on either side of the fence and ride it. When the Australians first started trying to soften up their image I thought it was a joke. A scientologist doesn't convert to Judaism.

Why would they bother, it's about winning, not being liked. Lots of people like Sri Lanka and New Zealand, how does that work out for them? Three or so years have passed since the Australian players signed their spirit of cricket nonsense and Australia's new nice guy tag still doesn't fit correctly. How could it?

Ponting is a street fighter. The working class boy who loves a scrap, and would smack you over the head with a chair to defeat you.
Hayden is a Christian soldier. Like Dubya Bush before him, he is an evangelical fighter who doesn't let knowledge or common sense affect his judgement.
Symonds is a black man from New Texas (Queensland); imagine the crap he has had to deal with his whole life. If that hasn't made him harder than a teenager in a nudie club, I don't know what would.
Hogg is six Tests into a career, has no real talent, and is sledging guys with over 5,000 Test runs. Imagine what he did to the dogs on his old postman's route.

Before them were men like Justin Langer, who I personally saw threaten at least three Victorians with violence. Steve Waugh, a man who believed in scarring the opposition for life and whose face broke Jason Gillespie's leg. And Allan Border, the man who told Dean Jones he was soft, as Dean Jones threw up in India while making a double hundred.

No, I wasn't one of the guys Langer threatened, I'm not that silly. In Aussie Rules football I barrack for Collingwood, everyone hates Collingwood. That's the way it should be. I couldn't stand it if I barracked for a side that provoked no reaction. I don't know why this team decided to be liked, but I can only imagine it had something to do with making fat cash off sponsors.

Personally I think they make enough cash from cricket, so they should concentrate on winning cricket matches. If they really want to do something for their image, they can always do what Steve Waugh did, feed the starving limbless children. Didn't matter that Steve would have strangled an Indian to win a Test on the pitch, because he did nice things off the pitch.

India would love to be two-zip right now; Bangladesh would love to win two Tests.

Australia aren't ever going to be completely nice, cause it ain't in them. So let's drop the act gents, if nice guys finished first, we would have tried it already.

January 8 - Remember cricket, it's the thing they play between hearings and press conferences

A lot of people seemed to miss this, but while Australians were being hypocrites and Indians were throwing hissy fits, there was a Test that got played. I'm going to do something radical here and talk about the cricket.

Australia has two bowlers of Test match standard. Brett Lee, the reformed Indian singer, who has suddenly learnt how to combine bowling fast with taking wickets, and

Stuart Clark, the middle management specialist who just continues to take wickets. Then they have Mitchell Johnson, who has two personalities. One day he is a fire breathing dragon, the next a puppy with a wet nose. Luckily for him, Ricky Ponting seems to like him, which may account for the amazing amount of overs he bowled in the first innings, even when he continued to bowl dribble.

The last of the quartet is George Bradley Hogg, the man who is not talented enough to be related to the great north suburban fire-brand Rodney Hogg (Yes Googlers, Rodney Hogg is not Brad Hogg's daddy/uncle/cousin or husband). I never though he was up to Test match standard, and judging from the last afternoon in Sydney, neither does Ricky. Players who do not have full support of Ricky tend to go the way of Jimmy Hoffa. Mind you Ricky may not have to stomp his foot. Hogg is injured and under investigation, plus the selectors are dying to bring Tait in at the WACA.

Their batting is quite solid, but there is one major question mark: Michael Clarke. No one doubts this guy can seriously bat, but he does struggle under the strenuous nature of coming in when wickets are falling and the pressure is at its hottest. He is a long way from being an automatic selection in my eyes.

India too have their problems. I love Yuvraj Singh the One Day player. Arrogant, clever, stylish, brutal. A run machine capable of taking apart a bowling attack piece by piece and mailing it back to its family in some sort of sick game. But I hate Yuvraj the Test player, frightened, lost, alone, cold, blocked sinuses. A scrawny man at a Xena Warrior Princess convention. Where is the Yuvraj I know and love, 'cause this one stinks. Wasim Jaffer can bat, I am positive of this fact. Unfortunately right at the moment, he is not. As I write this he is on the street in front of his hotel, waving his bat at cars and expecting them to magically swerve and not hit him. Perhaps in the second dig Rahul Dravid again found some semblance of form, but the WACA will test that out once and for all.

Setting aside what happens to Harbhajan, the fourth bowler is the only concern for India's attack. But that said Sharma is a shoe-in for Perth, I mean what is this guy, like eight feet tall.

Remember when we used to talk about cricket all the time, back in 2007? It seems like only yesterday.

January 9 - If only Andre Nel had a moustache

Against my better judgment, I really like Andre Nel. Then again, I have always been partial to mass murderers and cult leaders, so maybe he just continues that trend for me. Frequent readers of this site may be confused, as Nel is South African, and judging by my previous record, I'm not their biggest fan. Try as I might, I just can't help but like him.

Andre is the sort of guy you would love to have on your team. He gives it everything he has, and when that doesn't work, you can sit at first slip and piss yourself while he rolls around the ground after beating a tailender with a straight one. Clearly he is insane, I wouldn't argue with that.

If I had to watch a fast bowler late at night, after a few lagers, on my couch, with Natalie Portman beside me, there is no one else in the modern game I would prefer to watch. We all know the strain of professionalism is killing entertaining cricketers, and in bowling, the situation is particularly grim. The life seems to have disappeared from them, as Probot (professional robot cricketers) bowlers and toilers are taking over.

While watching probing overs from Stuart Clark, my mind wanders to thoughts about self-mutilation. When Matthew Hoggard grunts in, I wonder why I spend so much time watching this game. And if I have to deal with another Kiwi grinder chugging in for a long spell, I might go postal, or worse, become a scientologist.

That's why I love Andre, he is completely different from the current crop of fast bowlers, other than his protégé Sreesanth. I love it when he gives a vicious outburst for what seems a fairly common occurrence, i.e. a two minute spray for a batsman missing an outswinger. His exaggerated follow-through for every ball. The way he turns fast bowling into performance art. His amazement in not getting a wicket every ball. The look on his face when a batsman has the audacity to hit a four off him, or a single. The fact he has a hot sister who likes chubby balding cricketers. When he dropped Allan Donald with a bouncer, and cried about it. That he has been caught drink driving and using weed.

He is also underrated as a bowler, as the man is a perfect first change bowler. He is tall, hard to play, always at you, can move the ball both ways, and has a more than handy bouncer. If you told him to bowl up hill, into a gale, while it rained, on a road, with a midget on his back, he would do so. You can't find many people like that; most bowlers frown at the word midget.

I think the best thing about him is that he makes the batsman assume he is a raving loony. Another man did this: his name was Merv Hughes. While they laugh and scoff at his antics, his brain is ticking over with a new plan to get them out. When they don't take you seriously, they forget you're a threat. Here's to the high class buffoonery of Andre Nel.

Let's hope like hell there is never another quite like him, (as Scotland Yard don't need the extra work), but that there are several who are just as insane without the homicidal maniac bit.

January 9 - Lord Megachief of Gold & the Imaginary Girlfriend Sex theory

Continued coverage of the Windies tour in South Africa.

One day I will write a really positive article on Shivnarine Chanderpaul, but today is not that day. Sometimes in life you need to do things for the Greater Good. It's like if you have a girlfriend, and you think all her friends are pretentious wankers, and she asks you to go to a party at one of their houses. By not going to said party, you may anger your girlfriend, and sex may be withheld from you.

So even though you don't want to spend a minute with these people, you understand that a few hours with them will give between one and two minutes of pure dirty lust-filled joy with her. Shivnarine needs to understand this principle. We know that he doesn't want to captain the Windies: he quit that job to concentrate on his batting. This has worked out quite nicely for him.

With Gayle injured, Sarwan not available and Frank Worrell dead, surely Shiv would have said, look, I don't want to do this, but I understand that for one game, and one game only, I am the man who should lead my country, you know, for the Greater Good.

I would have thought, however incorrectly, that this is a sure thing to happen. Apparently not. Instead Dwayne Bravo is going to be captain, sure he is vice captain, but that was chosen to give his game focus, and surely not because he was giving invaluable tips to Chris Gayle. In the field of the last two Tests I have hardly seen Gayle chat to Bravo. I think Bravo is a gun player, who probably needs stick and carrot type handling, but being that he is 24 and has played in one Test victory, and Chanderpaul is almost as old as Bryce McGain and has played in over 100 Tests, for this occasion perhaps Shiv might have been the better option.

I hope I'm wrong, cause if I'm wrong, South Africa might lose the series, and I will dance for 12 minutes straight if that happens. But I won't be getting my dancing shoes out just yet. With Gayle out and Edwards doubtful, I can't see the Windies winning.

January 10 - Graeme – the new pop idol

It may come as a shock to you, but India and Australia are not the only Test nations on earth. I have just watched something that makes me feel ill. Graeme Smith making a hundred. I'm sure some of you have seen this before, it doesn't happen often, recently anyway, but this is not the first time.

The man was in worse form than the 40-year-old virgin, and all of a sudden he starts picking on the Windies. Why? Because he can't pick on anyone else. It takes a special kind of opening batsmen to average 30 in Test cricket over the last two years, with the opening bowlers we have in international cricket. And by special I mean crap.

Certain people may not like Matthew Hayden cause he averages over 50 against opening attacks that would struggle to get Mike Whitney out, but at least he consistently make runs against all countries around the world. He is a consistent bully, and with the exception of Shoaib Ahktar, there is no one bowler that really troubles him. Smith talks like a bully, is built like a bully, probably smells like a bully and certainly wants to be a bully, but he lacks the actual runs to do so.

He is the epitome of what is wrong with the South Africans. They are great at smashing average teams, out of form teams, and minnows (that was not a Kiwi joke) but when the heat is really on we all know Graeme Smith will not be up to the challenge. They still gloat about breaking the world record run chase against Australia.

It didn't happen in a World Cup, so who cares. Lots of people hold records, I held one in a call centre for mentioning a customer's name over 24 times in a minute. Didn't win me a World Cup though. Australia intrinsically knows that when a major game is played against South Africa, South Africa will fail.

Runs against the Windies may prop up your average, they may even make you feel like you're hitting form, hell you may even think your penis is larger, but they are as important as winning a pop idol show, and Graeme, you look fat in that dress.

January 12 - Another red nut bites the dust

Shaun Pollock has retired. Yawn.

I checked my previous posts to see how many times he has been mentioned on Cricket With Balls. There was two, one was by infrequent contributor Sime and it said "Old man Pollock (Shaun) was in the dressing room, in between stints as a substitute fielder, plotting his second cricketing life, as a wicket keeper, donning the gloves in what can only be described as a bizarre piece of footage from the player's balcony".

The other was my post, Shaun Pollock of the dead, which was hated by most people. Especially people from the BBC site I placed it on, which is probably why I like it. In this post I mention that he had almost no impact on me, and since I've written over 400 blog posts now and mentioned him twice I think you get the idea. He didn't even make my post about evil South Africans.

He is a eunuch, he is beige, he is platonic, he is a pop star, he is a fibre-enriched breakfast cereal, and if he didn't have red hair, I may have never even noticed him. Everyone has a story about how they saw him do something great once, except for me; perhaps I slept through it. My problem with him is that at no stage did I ever feel like he was pushing his talent as far as it could go. I always felt like he was holding himself back, like there was more to give, but that he felt comfortable with his efforts.

He played like a Proboter (professional robot cricketer), when he could have been anything. Who does that? I wasn't born with his talent, but if I was, and I played my cricket as a medium paced handy batsmen I'd be fuckin' horrified with myself. In his retirement speech he said he thanked God for his talents. Well Shaun if I was God, which is a possibility, I'd smite thee from this here land for eternity.

Fancy mentioning God when you play cricket like a scientologist. I am in the minority here; I can already see other people calling him a great, a brilliant flame haired superstar who was a phenomenal all rounder. The Pro Shaun Pollock movement will mention his amazing statistical record as proof of his greatness. Well if that's the case, Mike Hussey must be the second best batsman of all time.

I'm used to being in the minority, (not racially, or sexual preference wise, but politically and in my liking of Ian Harvey), and I choose to forget Shaun's career.

January 13 - Are the West Indies the new Tori Spelling

Marlon Samuels just scored his first hundred in five years; 2002/03 against India was the last. Let me tell you about five years ago: I was dating a girl who had not yet faked a pregnancy or told me she was about to kill herself in order to win me back. George W Bush had not yet invaded Iraq. Shaun Pollock was captain of South Africa. The last Matrix film hadn't come out. Paris Hilton wasn't famous. Jacques Kallis had hair. Aravinda de Silva still played cricket. Woody Allen lived in New York. Rupert Murdoch was Australian. Mel Gibson was a closet Christian. Sime was a fish and chip magician, and Big Daddy was single.

Also back then a young kid by the name of Marlon Samuels looked like he could be the next big thing from the Windies. Five years on, and the Windies are now only better than Bangladesh and the Kiwis (debatable, but going on form in South Africa).

Their captain bats like a drunk Canadian woodchopper. Their best batsman is a man who seems to have had enough of carrying his pathetic team-mates. Their gun all rounder is a derringer. Their bowling is less predictable than Robin Williams. And the rest of their batsmen are grade cricketers who got lost on their way to real jobs.

The Windies are really really really shit. Tara Reid shit, Celine Dion shit, TORI SPELLING SHIT.

Their only hope in not being the worst real Test nation is if New Zealand can't field a team, which by my estimations will happen in 2011. The worst thing was they got up our expectations by winning a test in South Africa, nothing could wipe the smile off my face, well until the second Test started and they got flogged.

Will that be the last Test win they have away from home?

January 14 – You, sir/madam/hermaphrodite, are a bastard of a monkey

Warning: this blog contains references to all sorts of really offensive stuff, so if bastard monkeys offend you, please step away now, or I'll throw a fatherless banana at you.

The title of this blog could mean different things to different people. To some it could be questioning the parentage of a black man. To others it could be something you say to a friend of yours who is a primate.

We live in tricky times. Political correctness is the new black. Hence why I haven't been asked to write for Cricinfo. There are certain things you can say to certain players that you can't say to other players. Like, you can't call Makhaya Ntini or Andrew Symonds a monkey, but you can call Steve Harmison one.

You can call an Australian a motherfucker, bastard, arsehole, cunt, shithead or poofter, but don't mention monkeys, just stay away from any primates. Don't call the Prime Minister of New Zealand a man. Don't call Ian Thorpe a big foot or a homosexual. And don't call a South African Muslim a terrorist.

You can call Brett Lee a man. You can call Elton John a homosexual with or without big feet. And you can call me a terrorist.

This is what confuses people. So I have devised a new plan: everyone is to be called by their number and their number only. If you don't have a number, I suggest you come up with one. My number is 3113455513 and that is all you are ever allowed to call me. My number has no racial connotations, cannot be called homosexual, isn't a monkey or a bastard, doesn't wear women's underwear, won't do ice, hasn't plotted the downfall of the Western civilisation, can't eat tofu or vote Republican.

Let us do a role play: lets say you're number 67342334, and I beat the bat with an inswinger that spat up past the edge of your bat like a cobra. I may walk down and say "you fucken lucky 67342334". You look back at me and say "you're such a little 3113455513, get back to your mark and bowl the fucken ball 3113455513, before I smack you upside your head". And then we laugh, and buy each other fried pig snacks and no one has to talk to Mike Proctor ever again.

Isn't that a world we all want to live in 67342334, by the way 67342334 your hair looks great today, no that's not what I meant, no, um sorry, I had no idea, no really that is not necessary, please don't get upset, I just meant, I'm sorry, put down that chair 67342334, please don't kill me, I'm way too beautiful to die...............

January 17 - Is swing bowling Australia's kryptonite?

This was in response to Australia struggling with the swinging ball in Perth, a Test India would go on to win and in which swing bowling was a major factor.

Swing bowling has been around for a long time. The Demon Fred Spofforth used it. And I'm sure the English had an opening bowler who perfected it before Rasputin was a boy. My point is that swing is not a new phenomenon. Australia has even had bowlers that practise the art, Bob Massie, Terry Alderman, Alan Davidson and Ricky Ponting among them. However, when a ball is delivered towards them, and it swings, in either direction, in either fashion, Australia tend to miss, nick or slice it. It is a worrying thing.

I even have evidence. Mind you it's evidence from my memory; it's not based on facts or anything.

Case 1, Ashes in 2005.

You could blame McGrath's ankle, Ponting's odd decisions, Warne's dropped catch, Rauf's hatred of Martyn, but to me the real reason was Australia's absolute capitulation to the swinging ball, reverse mostly, but occasionally traditional as well.

Case 2, Ben Hilfenhaus.
Tasmania won the Sheffield Shield last year. Sure they had some handy batsmen and an all rounder who played an amazing final, but simply put, Hilfenhaus averaged over six wickets a game bowling outswing. It was almost as if no one in Australia could play him.

Case 3, Agit Agarkar
He once took wickets in Australia.

I thought the reason we switched from Platypus balls to Kookaburra balls was to stop international teams from swinging the ball. Perhaps we need a new ball, the Echidna? Emu? Wombat?

January 17 - Once in a generation teddy bears

How many once in a generation players do Australia have at any one time? Four, maybe five. If Mitchell Johnson and Shane Watson are once in a generation, then surely Michael Clarke isn't all that once? So why is he being protected?

Are his five hundreds in 32 Tests enough to bat at number five for Australia? Apparently so. What if two of those five hundreds came in his first three Tests? So that's three hundreds in 29 Tests. An average of 43, not a lot for Australia's top order. That's half the average of the King Probot Michael Hussey, statistical anomaly that he is (proof of the Matrix?).

Are the Australian selectors wooed by his pretty shots and stunning footwork? I know I have been before, but now I look beyond the physical, I'm looking for an emotional connection based on trust, and Pup is not giving it to me. When Clarke walked to the wicket for his last three hundreds, Australia has been 4/257, 4/357, and 3/216.

Not exactly a tight rope pressure cooker hot in the kitchen type situation. The last eight times Clarke has come to the wicket with pressure on (four for less than 150, or three for less than 100) he failed to make a 50. Most times he has failed to make 20. Yes I looked it up. I do that from time to time.

I understand he has a hot missus, but so did Lyle Lovett, but that didn't really work out well for him. When wickets are falling he never stops the flow. Batting behind him is a man (Symonds) who no sober person ever thought would make a Test cricketer, yet right at the moment he looks ten times more reliable than Clarke.

In fact on form he should definitely be batting ahead of him. I know the rules are different for NSWelsh cricketers, but he's keeping out two things the selectors love, having two brothers in the side or having the captain of NSWales in the side. Three hundreds in 29 Tests should not be enough to keep Future PM David Hussey or the previous chosen one, the Krab Katich, out of the side.

No one doubts that Michael Clarke could be a sensational batsman, but shouldn't he be picked on runs on the board, not because pundits think he will take over as captain? I may even be getting ahead of myself because he has made three tons in the last eight Tests, but since none of them were under wicket pressure it's hard to rate them too highly.

Recently when he bats under pressure, even against Bangladesh, he fails. I didn't even know the Play-Doh Tigers knew how to assert pressure. He would not be the first Australian batsman to be dropped for continuing to fail under pressure, whilst making runs when the pressure is off. Dean Jones was another.

Symonds is finding his way, Gilly is nearing the end, and Brett Lee is not an all rounder. Australia cannot afford to carry any batsman. His role as Ponting's stuffed animal is vital, but we can get Ponting other toys to play with. Johnson perhaps; Ponting does like once in a generation toys, reminds him of his youth.

I hope he comes good, because in a world of Probots he is a wonder to watch, but he doesn't win matches and he doesn't save them. So the question would be, what does he do? Anyone?

January 19 - India win at WACA, Flintoff still drunk

I never congratulate Australia for winning, so it seems odd to do it for India. They beat Australia, which should be the aim of any team playing a Test. They trained hard, the conditions helped, the injury to Hayden helped, and they out-played Australia, and this led to a Test win. In order for India to become a great Test nation they should have expected to win this Test. Not because their fans expected to, but because they put in the hard yards, are a talented group of players and because they should believe in themselves.

India has the best record against Australia of any country over the last 15 years. And they were still two-nil down against this new look, obviously more frail Australian side. This is the side that almost lost a Test against one player (the king Kumar Sangakkara) in Hobart, only a few months ago. They kept out Clark and Lee as best they could. They worked over Hussey and Ponting pretty well, the pitch suited them more than it did Australia, and they found out Australia's dirty little secret: they ain't as good as they used to be.

India deserved to win the Test, but they must remember that all they have done is won one Test. England are still paying for thinking all their hard work in beating the Aussies was enough. Sure a bunch of them got (practically) knighted, and Freddie Flintoff is still drunk, but at the end of the day a win in one series is just a win in one series.

India hasn't done that. They have climbed a huge mountain in beating Australia at the WACA, but when they got to the top of the mountain, guess what they saw? Higher peaks. England saw that, and thought 'bollocks to that, let's go get a beer'. The Indian side is very well suited to beating Australia. Swing bowling and a formidable batting line-up is what England used. They are hungry and mostly in good form. They have good balance and used sound plans to bottle up Australia's gun batsmen.

Adelaide is a different fish of kettle. The ball may not swing, the Indian batsman may not be able to hold Lee and Clark out, and Hayden might come back. Plus the fact that pretty much since India drew in Australia four years ago, every time Australia has lost, they have played their best cricket. Look at their record after the 2005 Ashes, or their form at the World Cup after losing to England and New Zealand.

Then what? A score-line of three-one and the world seems a dark place again.

India must look at this win for what it is, a small step in the right direction, but many an explorer has fallen off a mountain. Even sober. And for all the other Test nations that thought this win means you will knock off Australia, remember these two details. The last time India toured they drew with Australia, and yet Australia has lost only one series since then. The last time Australia lost a Test was in 2005, and that got them so angry they went on a warpath demolishing all teams in their wake, and inspiring this 16 Test run.

Are they as good as they used to be? Of course not. Are they still good? Yup.

January 20 - Anil of the absurd

I have spent many hours looking at Anil, and I still can't understand how he gets wickets. I bowled a lot of straight leg spinners, and most of them got slogged over mid wicket, some to square leg. Not once did a coach say to me, hey shit cunt, you bowl alright, but you're spinning the ball a bit much, hold back and bowl some straight ones. I don't understand David Lynch films either; everyone is weird, the music is odd, the plot makes no sense, but at the end of the film I like what I've seen. Same as Kumble.

Of all the great modern spinners he is the one against whom you'd back yourself to get through an over. You probably wouldn't, but compared to Warne or Murali, you wouldn't be completely embarrassed either. You would miss the straight one though. Some people don't consider him a spinner, but some people don't consider Donnie Darko a modern classic.

Were it not for his constant wipes at that sweaty forehead, you would wonder if he were truly a human. I mean, what sort of a spinner bowls that many balls on a good length, with grace, patience and no spin?

Steve Waugh always says you wouldn't lose sleep the night before facing Kumble. This is probably true, but the night after facing him many a batsman has looked at the ceiling of a Delhi hotel thinking, "how the fuck did I miss another straight one".

He is not so much a bowler, but an artist who uses minimalism to deceive you. Like Samuel Beckett he strips away the reality of spinners needing to turn the ball a mile. He brings bowling back to the very base level of the human condition. Kumble turns batting into an introspection of life itself. The batsman has many questions to face during his spell.

Do I go forward, do I go back, is it turning, is it going straight, should I attack, should I defend, when is the right time, is he a leggie, is he an inswinger, can I pick his wrong 'un, is my penis really satisfying my partner?

A normal bowler tries to beat the batsman, but Kumble makes you define the very idiom of batsmanship. Then he bowls the straight one. Trust me, it is very hard to bat while thinking about idioms, especially when Kumble is probing at you with minimalism. Off the field he handles himself with a confident quiet calmness, part James Bond, part Riche Benaud, but Indian. He is smooth, classy, clever, respected and dignified at all times. Then he bowls the straight one.

Don't try and understand the straight one; just accept it for what it is, another wicket to the great man.

January 24 - Is Gilly a goner?

By this stage Gilly's keeping had hit an all time low, and you could sense he was on his way out.

According to Rodney Hogg, Adam Gilchrist can leave the game whenever he wants to. I have never ever believed crap like that. Champion players should get more leeway than other plays, no doubt, but the side is always more important than the player. Right now Gilly is struggling for form with the bat.

His career record is not great against India, but people think he bats well against them because of one knock. Sure it was the sort of knock you'd watch instead of having sex with Russian twins, but it was still only one knock. India is the only side against which he averages fewer than 40.

He just made a match-winning score in the World Cup final, albeit with the aid of a little black ball, so his form is not Shane Watson bad. It's his form with the gloves that is most troubling. He is dropping catches and missing stumpings. That's less than good. Bert Oldfield is turning over in his grave, but maintaining his soft hands.

Mind you, he has never been a superstar keeper; I cringe when people refer to him as a great keeper. As an all rounder he is a better keeper than, say, Jacques Kallis is a bowler, but his keeping is not of Imran Khan bowling level. If that makes sense. Boucher and Gilchrist may be the premier wicketkeepers in the world, but they don't really rate against even the most recent generation of wicketkeepers like Khan, Healy, Russell, and Richardson.

Gilchrist may have changed the world of cricket for ever. Positively, by batting in a manner that has inspired all teams to score quickly and take on attacks. Negatively, by ensuring all Test teams have batsmen who wear gloves.

Right now Australia is not in a position to allow the selection of a keeper who regularly misses chances. I'm not saying we drop him straight away, but surely the selectors must make him aware that getting 20 wickets for the new team is not as easy as it used to be. So he either starts taking the chances or he starts posing for a sculptor.

He is older than Bryce McGain, who is older than Jesus, so retirement is not the worst thing that can happen to him.

January 25 - Carpet bombs aren't funny, and neither is he

In 2007 I had been very disappointed that Brad Hogg was selected to play Test cricket, and by 2008 it was an all-consuming rage.

Ok the joke has gone on long enough. Apparently it's been April Fools Day for three Tests now. You may remember my constant (eight) posts saying he just wasn't up for it. It's not his fault. He wasn't going to say to the selectors, "hey I'm not really all over this Test bowling caper, and perhaps you should look elsewhere". He didn't ask Warne to retire, Stuey to get overweight, the Cullens to be shit or for McGain to be Victorian; these things just happened and he was promoted to the Australian Test team.

He is probably more surprised than the rest of us to be a Test bowler in the number one rated side on Earth. Every time the ball is thrown to him he probably starts to shine it, before someone whispers that he is expected to bowl with it. But please selectors, fuck him off. Send him back to his postal route, kick him out of the team hotel, give him some frequent flyers miles, hire a hit man to whack him, or feed him cocaine and drug test him the next day.

It's all fun and games until someone gets hurt, and we are all very fucken hurt right now. Because we Australians can't take this anymore. In this series he has bowled 110 overs, for seven wickets. Symonds and Clarke have bowled 98 for 14 wickets. He is half the bowler two part timers are.

How shit is that, seriously work it out, how shit, he is really shit, like seeing a wart growing on your pecker, or swallowing a fly over and over and over again type shit. Like watching Battlefield Earth sober type shit. I mean if Ganguly wasn't a fruit loop, he might have only three wickets in this series.

That's like getting your testicle or sensitive girl bits caught in a zipper shit. I am starting a petition for all Australians: George Bradley Hogg must go. Bring in Tait underdone, bring in an injured Hilfenhaus, and bring in Bracken and his sister's haircut, hell, even bring in Daniel Marsh. Anyone but Hogg.

You can even go retro. Get Tim May a suit that fits, allow Shane Warne a room full of skanks, bail out Terry Jenner, pick Gavin Robertson from club cricket, give Richie a bucket load of anti-aging cream, help me re-animate Tiger Bill or even turn back to Ray Bright or Greg Matthews, if worst comes to worst.

Because Brad Hogg is not a Test cricketer. Don't tell us he is improving, that he played to the game plan, that his batting is handy, that his pants fit nicely, that he gives good head, that the players like him, that all spinners struggle against India, just put him in a box and send him somewhere.

The West Bank perhaps. Sierra Leone is nice at this time of year. Or perhaps Kenya needs a new leggie.

Our enemies are enjoying this. From sportsfreak.co.nz: "Have you any idea how much I'm enjoying Hogg's "performance" over the last couple of days?". If the Kiwis, with a team full of civil servants, are laughing at us, what would teams with actual cricketers be doing? Do you know what England's strategy next Ashes is? Ensure Hogg is picked. I know I've been subtle in this post but I want to make sure the selectors understand my message.

GET RID OF THE TONGUE OR I WILL CARPET BOMB YOUR HOUSE YOU USELESS MOTHERFUCKERS.

PS, if somehow he takes wickets in the second innings, however unlikely that is, I was only taking the piss.
PPS, that line was added in case the Feds decided to charge me with any of the 43 terrorism offences I just committed.

January 29 - Turn around, every now and then

Remember the name Jason Krejza; it may come back again.

Apparently Shane Warne has retired. So the Australian team needs to find some spinners capable of taking wickets in Pakistan and India. Let's look at the list of contracted and uncontracted spinners.

Contracted

Stuart "Lord Stuey" MacGill is the enfant terrible of the private school leg spinning set. Currently injured and more interested in filming odd ads about wine, but is married to a hot chick. Has over 200 wickets, but has bad knees and is late 30s. May play again, but it looks doubtful, and even if he does he has worse knees than my grandma, and hers are fake.

Brad "the tongue" Hogg is the part time bowler who accidentally became a Test match spinner. Was once a postman, still bowls like one, and is a very effective weapon in One Day cricket, but is just not a Test cricketer. People say he is a nice bloke, but I don't think that is helping him take wickets in Test match cricket. His bowling average of 50 is not gonna keep him in the big time.

Dan "sleeves" Cullen took 40 wickets one year for the South Australian Redbacks. Since then he would be lucky to have taken 40 combined. Has played one Test against Bangladesh, and has a very annoying habit of scrunching his sleeves up before every fucking delivery. Was relegated to 12th man for the Redbacks' last game. Nowhere near the level needed to be playing for Australia.

Cullen "the other guy" Bailey is the saviour of leg spinning. So at the moment he is being crucified by not playing. Right at the moment he is the highest paid club cricketer in the land. Hasn't been picked for first class cricket in four months. Not even his father the preacher can save him now.

Uncontracted

Cricket With Balls' own Nice Bryce McGain is the pin-up athlete for the blue rinse brigade. Sure he is slightly older than the usual debutant (cough57cough), but he does this weird thing: he gets wickets. If he wore a lighter shade of blue he'd probably be playing right now, or perhaps the selectors don't like Hugh Grant films. He is the best spinner in Australia at the moment, unless my plan to re-animate the corpse of Tiger Bill O'Reilly has been successful.

Aaron "Billy" Heal is the child of a bastard union between Billy Bowden and Mr Squiggle. Ok, he can't get a game for his state, but he did bowl very well against Sri Lanka in a tour game. That's not the greatest rap for him, but he does look like a bowler, and if he played on a wicket that helped spinners we may actually know how good he could be. In the One Day and Twenty20 comps he has bowled really well, and Sime likes him and Sime doesn't like anyone with fewer than 250 Test wickets.

Jason "who?" Krejza is some guy who plays cricket I suppose. He is the leading finger spinner statically at the moment. That's like being the tallest dwarf though. His greatest asset is the fact he can bat, probably too well, as he plays quite often as a part time spinner and full time number eight. He has wickets though, so that is something.

The Skinny this summer

McGain has taken 24 wickets at 33. Hogg 20 wickets at 40. Krejza 13 wickets at 35. Cullen 11 wickets at 50. Bailey, Heal, and Stuey aren't really worth mentioning.

Australia's spinning stable hasn't been this ugly since Terry Jenner went to the big house.

January 31 - Gilly

This is my sixth attempt at writing about Gilly's retirement. There were some good ones and some shit ones in there, but none of them felt right. But in the spirit of Gilly, I thought fuck it, just swing away.

Gilly batted like all of us wished we could. With power and without fear. On the ground he was like a Spartan, dispatching mere mortals and inspiring fables the world over. The balls it takes to bat like Gilly, even once in a Test match, are pretty big, but to do it for a whole career and be successful is obscene.

The man had a set of balls that could sink a battleship and he batted in a way that would have given Lucifer an erection. Do you know how hard it is to be thought of as cool, when you have a ten-year-old's hair cut, ears four sizes too big and a nice guy demeanour? But not much about Gilly made sense. While others were tentative, he threw his bat at the ball like it was a cheating wife in the suburbs, ok bad example, but you get my point.

It was almost as if the ball was the enemy, and the bowler was just another faceless drone delivering it to him. When the best were good, they could trouble him, Akram and Freddie Flintoff especially, but when he stood up to them, they looked meek in comparison. He made cricket a game where batsmen were the aggressors and bowlers were abused. With gloves on he became mortal again, but with the bat in hand he was Muhammad Ali, he was Lee Marvin and he was as brutal as any man before him, and probably any man to follow.

Calling him a great of the game is almost understating it, he not only played the game, he changed the game, and not too many people end up with that on their headstone. Thanks Gilly, for the cricket and everything else.

Cricket is a better-looking lass for having danced with you.

February 2 - You tell 'em champ

Graeme Smith has abused Andrew Symonds and Harbhajan Singh for losing respect for the game. Apparently he did so with a straight face. At the same time he praised former leader Hansie Cronje for finding Jesus. Then he said that Gibbs and Boje have an allergic reaction to Indian food, but surprisingly Bangladeshi and Sri Lankan food was fine. He also went on to say that Tony Greig was a good bloke and Andre Nel was the sort of chap you'd want dating your sister.

Smithy thought that India and Australia should take a leaf out of South Africa's book and all their problems would be solved. Race issues are very important to Graeme Smith, because his cook, maid, driver and security guard should all be allowed equal rights. After the press conference he got a great shoe shine. Personally I believe racism could be solved if all people, male and female and other, looked like Rosario Dawson.

February 4 - Replacing Gilly with a human

Wicketkeepers are great. No really they are. Australia is losing one, so it is now their turn to look into the pantry cupboard to see what there is on the shelf.

Brad Haddin is the breakfast cereal that is marketed as "tastes great and is good for you". In other words you know that it's going to let you down one way or the other, you just hope it's not both. He can seriously bat, and he can catch the ball more often than not. Could possibly bat at six with someone like Ashley Noffke or Andrew McDonald behind him. He is the sound logical choice, so I'll look elsewhere.

Luke Ronchi is pancake mix. Sure homemade pancakes are better, but this is easier and your pancakes will come quickly. Negative point: his Kiwi heritage. Positive point: he hits the ball like it cheated him in a card game. Is good enough to get picked as batsman in the best domestic batting line up in the world. Only in Australia would he not be an automatic selection.

Adam Crosthwaite is the bag of chips; sure they taste good, but you can't eat them for five days. His keeping is top-notch, his batting is dyslexic. The other night he won a game off his helmet, and he is by far Victoria's best batsman under pressure. But a severe lack of runs means he is only an automatic selection in One Dayers and Twenty20. Is willing to cheat, which should be a pre-requisite for Australian keepers, especially after the last few years of the saint walker behind the stumps.

Chris Hartley is a Soda Fountain. In the 50s everyone had one, but not many of us have them now. The boy can seriously wicketkeep, but he can only just bat, and like Darren Berry before him he was born in the wrong generation. If John Howard gets re-elected and the world starts commie-bashing again, he may just wicketkeep for Australia.

And Tim Paine is like the expensive bottle of wine you put in the bottom of your pantry because you have no other room. It should still age well. Look, the boy isn't quite ready, but if the selectors want to make a Healy choice, which they won't, this is the man you would pick. He is a good enough batsman to open for Tassie, and it would be good for Australian cricket if a Tasmanian was in the Test team.

Paine is my choice; someone has to pick the kids.

February 6 - The perfect boyfriend

Women are weird, no doubt. They are harder to work out than HTML codes and what shoes are cool right now. In my travels I have met a lot of them, mostly through rejections, and I have come to learn some things about them. A great deal of women, which is now known as a vajority, want a man who can protect them from the elements while being gentle in those quieter moments on the couch. This is according to a female friend who said, "women want a man hard on the outside and soft on the inside." (This is obviously not all women, as the woman who repeatedly asked me to choke her wasn't so much into gentleness.) Unfortunately for me, I'm soft on the outside and hard on the inside. But Jacob Oram is hard on the outside and soft on the inside.

He bats like John McClane would. It isn't always pretty, there are some moments you aren't sure he is going to make it, and he ends up battered and bruised, but the bad guy is slain and we are kept entertained. When he bowls he shows a feminine side not many men his size can project. He trundles in like some sort of Oprah bowler, which is very different to being a Jerry Springer bowler like Andre Nel or Sreesanth. You could say he places the ball down with a softness unknown to most men his size.

This is what makes him the perfect boyfriend. To his mates he shows a tough guy demeanour, slogging the ball out of the park and carrying his decrepit team-mates on his back through another collapse. The sort of guy who would defend a lady's honour with a bloody bar fight. But after the bar fight, as the lady, whose honour is intact, is stitching him back up, he shows his sensitive side, as the alcohol and needles cause him to flinch and open up about past loves and scars that show just a hint of melancholy below his rock hard exterior.

Then they make sweet sweet love. He is gentle and giving, but as much as she enjoys it, some deep primal urge wishes that he would just rip her clothes off and make love to her in the wild abandon that he showed in the bar. Unfortunately for her (NZ), all his anger is reserved for bar room brawls (batting) and cannot be used in the making of love (bowling).

Ok so maybe not the perfect boyfriend then, but I bet he remembers her birthday.

February 7 - my retirement

In February it seemed like a lot of players with no hope of ever playing international cricket again were calling it quits, so I decided to do the same.

I have called this press conference to announce my retirement from international and first class cricket. I understand that I don't play international or first class cricket and that this is not a real press conference. Please hold all your questions 'til the end.

I realise that 28 is a very young age to announce my retirement, but I was prejudiced by the fact I have not yet played district cricket and therefore I see my promotion opportunities as slim to none. Also I would like to spend more time with family and friends, but for the next little while I may be busy with hookers and cocaine. My first class career, while non-existent, was still very fulfilling, and I'm sure, had I played, I would come to love my team-mates. Even Brad Hodge.

My international career was as illustrious as my first class career. Representing your country is an honour, and one that I will never cherish. Had I played I would like to think I could have convinced Ponting, through gentle jibes, that there is no need for artificial turf on top. I will not regale you with my career highlights, as you know them all, but I would like to thank my sponsors, the pizza bar, Cinema Nova and Blogger for their continued support over the years.

I'd also like to thank my wife, my mistress, her mistress, my children and the child I thought was mine but happened to be Michael Slater's, for the love they have given me.

I know some of you are sad, but you should know I am going out on top, and I know that it's time to move into the next phase of my life: filming home sex videos and going to jail for payroll fraud.

When thinking of retirement I was reminded of a conversation I had with Allan Border seven years ago. He said "how ya going?" and from that I sensed that one day I wouldn't be 'going well' and would know it was time to leave the international arena. I will continue to play cricket for the Whoseabouts indoor cricket team, for as long as I can catch public transport to the indoor centre.

I hope you will give me personal space during this transitional period. Thank you, oh and by the way, I see the sports media as the boil on the arse of humanity.

February 9 - Graeme is desperate and dateless

"It's kind of hard to go on one date, have a nice dinner and then say: 'That was nice - what are you doing in six weeks' time? I'm going to Chittagong." Graeme Smith in an interview with the Cape Times on why he is still single.

I'm not an expert on what ladies find attractive or not, but surely being the captain of your country, playing cricket professionally and travelling the world would entice some silly little girl into saying "I wuv you Smithy". The bigger question may be, is it possible to have dinner with Graeme Smith and for it to be nice? I suggest four reasons that could explain why Graeme Smith doesn't have a girlfriend.

One, because he is a homosexual. By calling Graeme Smith a potential man lover, I apologise to the whole gay community in the sincere way that Eminem did.
Two, because he likes to shag around, and who can blame him, it's the women who lower themselves that I blame.
Three, because he is a cunt.
Four, because he is a fucktard (©republiquecricket.com).

Seriously Graeme, in a world where Jacques Kallis went out with Cindy Nel and blokes like Lyle Lovett and Tom Green have dated Hollywood Royalty, I'm sure you can find some pathetic creature that is a blind deaf mute, with a limp, to share those cold and lonely nights in Chittagong.

February 10 – Batsmen need culling

This was following a One Day game during India's tour of Australia where 319 runs for 15 wickets were taken. Everyone blamed the pitch, but I worshipped it.

The G had grass on the wicket, so there was a different kind of One Day game played last night. You may remember this kind, where bowlers enjoy themselves. The Indian bowlers enjoyed themselves immensely and the Aussies ended up 150-odd. The Aussie bowlers were frothing at the mouth to get to the wicket, but when they got there they were too anxious, you know what I'm talking about ladies.

Most people don't like One Dayers when the bowlers dictate. But most people are idiots. My perfect One Day game would be one team making 184, and the other making 183 and Inzy getting run out. Perhaps I remember them fondly from my youth, or perhaps I'm a cricket sadist.

Batsmen get it all too easy these days. How else could you explain Sourav Ganguly and Graeme Smith? Flat decks, ropes in the outfield, hard replacement balls, and 20 over field restrictions are making batsmen look good. Who wants to see batsmen look good all the time?

I want to see them bleed, I want them to count their bruises at the end of a match, I want them to be stumped by four metres and then fall over in a final act of indecency. I want them to be publicly pantsed. I want them to be so angry they hit the dude who opens the gate for them. I want a batsman to go insane with rage and start a battle to the death with the bowler who has just got him out. I want wickets with more life in them than a Mormon. I want wickets who practice adultery, go to swingers parties, engage in public fornication and enjoy all the pleasures of anal sex.

I want Shaun Tait to come back and literally rip the throat out of some poor helpless English opening batsmen with a ball on a good length. I want Murali to spin the ball so far he has to land them off the cut strip. I want a ban on elbow guards, inner thigh pads, chest guards and any other nancy-boy protection. I want Tony Greig to be publicly executed for bringing 'crash helmets' into cricket. I want tailenders to think about how much they love their family before they get in behind a Dale Steyn delivery. I want batsmen to get hit on the first morning of a match, and to get bamboozled by spin of the last afternoon of a Test.

I want blood, carnage and wickets. I want to know a batsman can bat, not just watch him flay away bowlers on wickets flatter than an eight-year-old's chest. I want pain, lots and lots of pain, for batsmen and their families: mental, physical and otherwise.

I want bowlers to rule again.

February 10 - Adam don't like a badonkadonk

Jesse Ryder's debut on The Balls.

Adam Parore was a pretty handy keeper batsman for the Kiwis back in the day. He didn't set the world on fire, but he sure had some balls on him. If I remember correctly, he used to take an hour to face up to every ball. Sledging was his main focus in cricket, so he is someone I always admired. Now he is in the media, and he's still only a battler, but his sledging is top notch as per usual.

He is quickly becoming the new Neil Harvey/Bishen Bedi, which means no one other than journalists looking for a rent-a-quote will talk to him. Recently he has taken to bagging the new fat kid in town, Jesse Ryder. Bagging fat people is still in, it's below racism and sexism, so you don't get in trouble for saying it yet. His official words were, "Hey fatso, you're too fucking fat to play for the Kiwis, why don't you fuck off to Australia and do that old bird that Mark Waugh used to shag".

Not particularly nice, but it does have a lovely flow to it.

When Jesse was allowed to reply, it was hard to hear his response, as he had four Big Macs and a Subway 'eat fresh' seven foot long sub (with minus 3 grams of fat) in his mouth. But it sounded like, "Fucking Parore, that fucking arsehole, he's a fucking cunt and everyone knows it, betcha he didn't tell Greatbatch or McMillan to fuck off for being fat. No money in it for him, pass the fries will ya dude."

Good use of the word dude. Personally I think we should have more fat cricketers, who occasionally don't turn up for matches and threaten to play for other countries. That could only be a good thing for cricket.

I used to hate Jacques Kallis, but now he is fat, and balding, I only despise him, and I think I'm a better man for it. And for the NZ cricket administracrats it opens up a whole new world of marketing.

Jesse Ryder fat camps, attendance non-compulsory.
Jesse on Dr Phil.
Jesse's new single, Baby Got Back.
Jesse diet shakes, they give you the runs.
The Jesse Ryder workout video, with him clad in Spandex, eating burgers and scratching himself.

That is something we all want to see. Also, his first headline after making some runs is easy to write. Ryder's Appetite For Runs is Huge, Jesse Scores Big, Jesse's Huge Numbers, Jesse Devours Attack, Jesse is Big and Fat But he Sure Can Bat....

February 12 - Badonkadonk Ryder brushing dirt off his shoulder

Does everyone remember Notorious B.I.G. (aka Biggie Smalls), the fat rapper who was killed by 2pac, Suge Knight, the FBI and Tibetan monks? Of course you do. Well Jesse Ryder is the cricket version.

He got the swagger (ok more of a waddle). He got the confidence (winking at bowlers and smiling all the time). He got the game (well against the England he does). He got the rivalry (Parore). He got the dark past, (not as a teenage drug dealer, but he still got into shit). And most importantly he got the size (baby got back).

Everyone had an opinion on him before he even stretched out the black uniform. Too fat, loose cannon, unreliable, but Jesse does this thing that people like, he scores an arse-full of runs quickly. You see while the cricket academies teach nutrition and the best way to compile an innings, Jesse goes out there and hits the ball hard, scares bowlers and makes runs.

What an interesting cricket concept. Surely he should structure his innings around ten ball KPIs and not swing like he is in a fight over the last French fry. If you listen to John Buchanan or Ian Healy, cricket is a multilayered association of ideas that requires you to use all orifices at once whilst comprehending a series of numerical problems and remaining centred to the spirituality of your surrounds, and keeping your chi balanced.

Or you could be a fat party animal with a good eye.

Jesse Ryder is already a cult figure, figure being the key word. He was more popular than Shane Watson before he played a shot. Us armchair fans tend to like cricketers who don't look like male models. Jesse looks like he could sit comfortably in an armchair with a bucket of fried chicken and a bucket of cheap bourbon, so it is very hard to hate the man.

With Inzy, Lehmann, and McMillan gone, the hefty cricket fans need a new role model, and who better than Jesse. In the film Young Blood, Patrick Swayze says, "Thank God there is a sport for middle-sized white boys". Well if I was in a cricket film right now I would say, "Thank the aliens there is a sport for overweight drunkards".

February 14 - Hegemony or Fleming

Stephen Fleming's retirement post.

I think I once compared Stephen Fleming to Noam Chomsky. At the time I was just trying to sound intelligent. But now I look back, I realise I am a genius, and you should all listen to me more often.

Noam Chomsky is a leftist writer who uses big words and believes America is out to get him. Fleming used a left wing game plan, uses big words and generally thinks Australia is out to get him. Of course if Fleming was Chomsky, that makes Ponting George W Bush.

People either think Fleming is an overrated nerd who couldn't bat, or a tactical genius who almost took down the Australians and regularly won One Day games he shouldn't have.

I tend to think he was a genius, but I was a captain, and captains tend to rate captains more highly. What he did do was captain an extremely average side. Yet somehow under him New Zealand were never that bad. He never had the cattle to make a great team, he never had the hat to make himself a great cowboy, but he got the most out of himself and out of his team, and you have to respect him for that. Even if you think he was a shocking bat.

I wish there were more captains like Fleming, he captained like a mad scientist, rather than the McDonald's managers most captains are. Without guys like Fleming, cricket would still be stuck in the 1800s and we would all be bored shitless.

But for the average leftist person, Michael Moore's jokey easy style is a lot easier to follow than Noam's darkly multilayered manifestos.

February 15 Gilly's waltz

During Gilly's long goodbye campaign, he gave his home crowd a special One Day memento.

Adam Gilchrist decided to save one last dance for Perth. A gentlemanly hundred. It was a romantic gesture, but it would have been nicer if the game was on Valentine's Day. Interestingly enough, while Gilly usually tries to do the mash potato, this time he went with a waltz. Gilly is such a super guy, he wanted this one to last. One last jaunt around the dance hall for old time's sake.

He even got the DJ, Clarke, to put on some slow music, so it would last all night. Unfortunately, Gilly did what he has done all too often in his career, he made all the other men look like dodgy dancers. Hayden had two left feet. Punter was moving to the wrong tune. Symonds decided to spend time at the bar. And Hussey danced the Perth two-step, but he never really got the rhythm of it.

Gilly twirled around with a grace usually reserved for ballerinas or Muhammad Ali. Gilly has danced longer, faster, sexier and better many a time before, but this one had a certain sumthin' sumthin'. When the Sri Lankans hit the floor, only the King Kumar danced anywhere near as good, but he ran out of partners. Happens to the best of us.

Anything Gilly does from here on in is gravy. He can stumble, stand on feet, dance to the wrong song, or anything else, but his hometown crowd will remember this dance for a long time.

February 19 - Get David Hussey into office

David Hussey was continuing to make domestic cricket his own, and no more than in the white ball game, and since getting him elected Prime Minister didn't work, I took a stab at getting him in the One Day team. This petition got a couple of hundred signatures (comments).

The Australian One Day cricket team is struggling to make runs. These things happen; without Clarke or Gilly they might not have passed 200 runs yet. Ponting, Hayden, and Symonds have all looked muted. King Probot Michael Hussey has been ok.

But what would a normal cricket side do when its players are out of form? They would bring in a new player. The Australian team don't drop players, they rest them, retire them, name new squads without certain names in them, or wait for injuries. So rest them already. Bring in Future PM David Hussey. Hussey has been humping at the selectors' legs like a horny Labrador for years now.

There is not another cricket side in the world he wouldn't stroll into. New Zealand would gladly give up Helen Clark and Peter Jackson just to have him for two Tests against England. The West Indies would donate an island for him, tax free. And England would allow Kylie to come home just so they could slip him in behind KP.

This has gone on long enough. The team is not scoring, the batsmen look tired, and Symonds and Ponting look like they are carrying injuries, and yet all David does for Australia is collect frequent flyer points. And I worked for Qantas, trust me, they are impossible to use. So this is the petition, as suggested by Homer (dopaisekatamasha.blogspot.com), if you want David Hussey to play for Australia please sign your name in the comments.

Tell your friends, tell your enemies, hell, tell NSWelshman, but get the word out. Cricket With Balls needs your name on this petition and if we get over 1,000 people on the petition, I promise I will deliver it in person to Cricket Australia headquarters. This has gone on too long, and the only thing that will stop me from marching into the ivory tower of Cricket Australia is David Hussey representing Australia. Get signing people.

February 22 - My Application

Why should bloggers miss out on the IPL cash bonanza?

Dear Sir/Madam/IPL,
My name is Uncle J Rod, and I would like to apply for a position as blogger for one of your teams, preferably a team with a good name, so the Chennai Super Kings is out. Unlike all the other naysayers, I think Twenty20 cricket is the best thing since the up-skirt shot in Basic Instinct, although it is still no Barbarella.

These are some of the reasons I think I could fit into the IPL. I also don't think Ashwell Prince is very good. Talent-wise I am at least on par with Simon Katich. I have no problem with saying that India is the greatest nation on Earth, I mean I've lied before, I once told this girl her bum didn't look big in this. Also I will never place my feet near the Indian flag.

I have a work history of over 500 posts, most of which are not obscene. I have references from England, Pakistan, New Zealand (yes they are still a cricket nation) and India. None from South Africa though. I too hate the way Australia control world cricket, I mean look at the way they got that talented young finger chucker banned. Dharmasena I think his name was. For the job I am willing to do player interviews, players love me, I'm assuming you have heard of Bryce McGain.

Recently I started a petition to get David Hussey into the Australian side, and after only a few days I am only 900 people short of my intended target of 1,000.

I understand this is an auction process, but I would prefer to work with a team owned by a Bollywood actress. However, I am willing to work for any team where the groupie ratio is 25 to 1.

But I would like to reiterate I will not work for the Chennai Super Kings, as their name is really stoopid. I understand that a lot of money has been spent on the IPL, and you may be a little skint now, so I will make my reserve price 900,001 dollars, as I refuse to get paid less than Jacques Kallis.

In conclusion I am willing to declare all my other contracts null and void for the six week period where I will focus solely on making the IPL the greatest sporting event ever, except for the Melbourne Spring Racing Carnival and the WNBA.

Thank you for your time, and I hope to hear back from you shortly.

Yours truly,

Uncle J Rod

February 24 - Bryce – the wizard of oz

This was written about Bryce McGain's performance in the domestic One Day competition in Australia.

The game was a final. The game going, going, g......

Victoria had fallen apart with the bat, David Hussey aside. Dirty Dirk, Clinton and Harwood had done everything in their power for Victoria to win the One Day crown, but the rain and the circumstances were saying the game was over. The score had got to 5/109 chasing 131. I ain't no mathematician, but I'd say that's about 21 runs short. Cameron had lost a bunch of overs from his quicks thanks to Duckylewis.

Bryce was the only front liner left, and he hadn't bowled an over yet. Victorian leg spinners have a good record under pressure in finals, well one of them does. Bryce looked chubby, but that was because he was wearing four tops, as Tassie had turned very chilly.

Straight away he took a wicket; it wasn't a spectacular ball, it probably bounced a bit more than Diven thought and he skewed it to point. 6/109.

Still a long way from a victory, but there was something happening. Then two balls later he slides a ball past Xavier Doherty, who had a brain snap that would make OJ Simpson cringe. 7/109.

From there on in Bryce looked like he was bowling cluster bombs, one of which hit Geeves so straight in front Gilly and Jesus would have walked. Geeves didn't, and was given not out. Luckily for the Vics Dirty Dirk finally finished off Geeves and Bryce was left with Brendan Drew. 8/127.

Brendan is a big hitting tail ender, but against Bryce he looked like a drunken kitten. Bryce didn't have it all his own way with Drewy, the first edge he got was too sharp for Crosthwaite. Luckily enough next ball he got a more manageable edge straight into the centre of his gloves, Bryce is nothing if not considerate of others. 9/128.

Bryce only had two balls left against Hilfenhaus, the first was a probing nut right at him. Hilfy played it quite well. The next ball, McGain threw it wide, remember even Muhammad Ali makes mistakes, and Hilfy looked quite good while leaving the ball.

And that was it.

McGain had done everything he could do. Five overs. Two maidens. Three wickets (have not included Geeves due to bad LB call). 11 runs. The next ball was edged by Travis Turtle Birt, the dud Victorian who became the handy Tasmanian, and all of Bryce's magical tricks were forgotten as the Tasmanians danced around the ground.

The wizard was left to stroke his beard. BTW how cool would Bryce look with a long white beard?

February 25 - Killing kittens in kitchens

South Africa's tour of Bangladesh, where in some games Bangladesh seemed to push them.

South Africa are evil. Some may say they are evil dragons, but evil dragons are not this arrogant. The poor Bangladeshi kittens tried hard this week (not as hard as their dodgy curator did) and Shadadaadat Hossain took a bunch of wickets to make South Africa nervous. South Africa are not nervous now, they are sitting in a hot tub with various models of suspect intelligence, sipping on overpriced beers and telling each other what great blokes they are.

In December they lost a home test to the Windies, now they have been bundled out cheaply by Bangladesh. It would seem to all intelligent people that the minnows have them worried. This has not always been the case. In the past if the South Africans were playing with a minnow-type kitten, they would take off their military boot and smash its pretty little skull in. Then they would clean the boot, put it back on and leave a puddle of kitten brains and blood all over the kitchen floor.

In recent times, they seem to wanna play with the kitten for a while, see what makes it tick, tease it, make it think it might survive, and then give it an overdose of rat poison in its evening meal. You may think the boot idea is brutal, but at least the kitten doesn't suffer for long, and kitchen floors are easily cleaned. The rat poison death means the poor kitten thinks it has a chance of survival until it starts to cough up blood and think about everything it has not achieved in its adorably cute little life.

So I put it to you, Mr and Mrs Intelligent Person, that they, the evil South Africans, are not worried by the minnows, but have simply found a better way to torture small animals. The Evil Dragons would be appalled at this behaviour.

February 26 - Sydney – sooks & bullies

A month later after the bastard monkey affair Australia Vs India at the SCG inflames some tensions.

I think I've worked out exactly what is wrong with Australia vs India relations.

Sydney.

The Test series was fine, then Sydney came along. Australia started claiming one hand one bouncers, Bucknor found out Symonds was his long lost son, Anil Kumble lost his frame of reference, Harbhajan Singh and Symonds danced orally and Ishant Sharma "accidentally" got his gloves confused. Then World War Three started, it was like a particularly bad Bollywood film, without songs, terrible acting or happy endings.

Finally when bastard monkeys and Ricky Ponting's honour was no longer in question we started playing cricket in other states. The BCCI decided that the tour could continue, and the Test series was completed. Then Sri Lanka came out, no one could make runs, everyone except the batsmen seemed quite happy. Then a meaningless One Dayer in Sydney was played.

Dhoni used illegal gloves, Sharma asked Symonds to gently fuck off and the Australians are bullies again. I don't blame Dhoni for using illegal gloves. I don't blame Sharma for losing the plot. And I don't blame the Aussies for sledging until the Indians got caught retaliating.

I blame Sydney.

Not the BCCi and their sooky lala behaviour. Not Andrew Symonds and his well-bowled mates. Sydney, it can take non-sooks and non-bullies and make them Indians and Australians. Tony Greig lives there. Think of all the people who have been to Sydney and died: Kurt Cobain, John Lennon and Burt Reynolds. Also Tom Cruise likes Sydney.

The defence rests your honour.

February 26 - Stuey – it's time

Stuart MacGill's career was over, even if he didn't know it yet.

Let's be honest old fella, you've had a hell of a run. Literate types don't often play for Australia, so well done. How many cricketers pick a woman with brains and looks, kudos to you? Getting 200 wickets as an understudy is an exceptional effort. Your parents must be proud. Now you have a great career path mapped out with this wine company.

Your missus must make a nice packet, so you won't be out on the street for a while. This bowling caper, it isn't for a refined man like you, you've evolved, you're more of an after dinner speaker and wine sniffer these days. Bowling leg spin takes a modicum of physical fitness. It takes joints that are still capable of carrying your constantly bulging girth.

Cricket takes commitment, not to lifestyle programs, but to training. After all, leg spinning is a brutal art form, and if you aren't in gladiatorial shape, you best leave it to a young man. Like Cricket With Balls' Own Nice Bryce McGain.

February 27 - The tongue is gone

Brad Hogg's career was over, and he knew it, and thusly retired.

Like in Ichi the Killer or Oldboy, the tongue has been cut off, by its owner. This time however it has nothing to do with honour or having slept with one's daughter. Or has it….?

Brad Hogg has cited personal issues and "things he has to sort out at home" as his reasons for falling on his tongue. Apparently his wife is pregnant (Insert Michael Slater Joke Here). There are also rumours of him signing with the ICL. I'm assuming as a mascot. Brad Hogg was upset at having to leave the game, but in leaving he has strengthened Australia's Test bowling line up. With Stuey obviously finished, and Brad leaving, they both need new careers, and being the caring fellow I am, I think I have them covered.

They should move into a flat on the Gold Coast and film a soft-core porn mobile TV show called Spinners Gone Wild. Stuey can perform tricks with a bottle of red, and Brad does all sorts of fine work with his tongue.

Perhaps I should write about the career of Brad Hogg. He was selected as part of the experimental chinaman scheme that was started by Harold Holt. Michael Bevan and Simon the Krab Katich were also picked under this scheme. He was thrown into a tour of India because no one else wanted to be embarrassed, and then was picked again when Shane Warne was a drug cheat.

Having a career as an understudy (behind Shane) to the understudy (behind Stuey) would have bothered most men, but Brad Hogg never seemed to notice. He was just happy to be thought of as a cricketer (by selectors). As a One Day cricketer he was serviceable, and occasionally better than that, he had the amazing skill to look like he was bowling badly and still take wickets.

As a Test cricketer he was a train wreck. You have to respect him for getting the most out of so little; I don't, but you should. I would say that there has never been a spinner with less guile who has had a career this long, so that is something. George Bradley Hogg (no relation to the great Victorian speedster Rodney Hogg) you have had a career, good on ya.

But thank fuck you're gone.

February 27 - Army of one

Not enough cricket blogs reference Evil Dead films while talking about spinners.

CWB's Own Nice Bryce McGain is one step closer to victory over the army of skeletons. Spinners are falling down all around him.

The two young South Australians are almost irrelevant. "Are all men from the future loud-mouthed braggarts?"
The great Shane Warne has left the building. "Get offa me, ya crazy bitch!"
Brad Hogg has personal issues. "It's a trick, get an Axe."
And Stuey MacGill has retired, he just doesn't know it yet. "Well hello Mr fancy Pants."

So Bryce is pretty much the only one left. And that got me thinking of Army of Darkness. Perhaps because Bryce would look great with a chain saw as a hand. Or maybe because look the poster says,

Bryce is trapped by time (he'll be 48 next year).
Bryce is surrounded by evil (the selectors and NSWales).
Bryce is low on gas (not enough beans).

Bryce was initially mistaken for an old dude, but he was soon revealed as the prophesized saviour who can quest for a leggie, a delivery which can dispel the evil. He may not have a chainsaw as a hand, a chin made of granite or make snappy quips during action scenes, but Bryce is ready to fight the minions of darkness. There is no one left Bryce, please use your 20th century wits to save us from the deadites.

And feel free to throw in the odd "Yo, she-bitch! Let's go!" from time to time.

February 28 - Fine their organs

When I'm not pushing bandwagons for Bryce or getting people to sign David Hussey petitions, I'm trying to bring in a radical new punishment for slow over rates.

Castration. Any captain whose over rates are horrid should be castrated. Ricky, Anil, Daniel, all of them, there should be no exceptions. Even little Ashraful, who may not have even used his organ yet.

The latest captain to be fined for slow over rates is Graeme Smith. He lost 30% of his match fee, because his side had a shocking over rate against Bangladesh. It took forever to set fields against Bangladesh. Bangladesh. The same Bangladesh that made less than 380 runs in the match. How could these fields take to long to set?

Did I mention it was Bangladesh? South Africa were only in the field for 120 overs. Four sessions, and they still went over. Castration should be the minimum punishment for this indiscretion. And in the case of Graeme Smith, it's also a public service initiative for future generations.

February 29 - Bust a nut big man

The love affair may be over before it started. Badonkadonk Ryder has injured himself in a nasty bar room brawl with a toilet door. The door made no comment on the incident. He will need surgery to reconstruct his finger, three months in a padded cell and a skin graft. No jokes about where they will find any excess skin for said graft should be entertained.

The incident happened at 5 am, so there is a fair chance his night was just warming up and that he was sober. The toilet door, 24 of Christchurch, was accidentally locked, and Ryder desperately needed to drain a kidney after all the lemonades he had been consuming. Sprite has also declined to comment. The NZ Cricket Board are upset at the incident, although unnamed sources are just happy that no players signed up to the ICL overnight or got caught with weed.

Jesse has been under a lot of pressure recently; he was heard to say only days ago "Ya know it's hard out here for a pimp, with a whole lotta bitches jumpin' ship". Shane Bond and the Marshall boys had no comment either. The Kiwi administracrats must be worried about Ryder; he seems to have way too much personality to play cricket for New Zealand, and this kind of unruly behaviour is usually only tolerated in rugby players.

The ICL however have downgraded their offer to Ryder from $400,000 a year to $300,000 a year, but a promotional deal with Cuervo has been struck up for Ryder in Goa, so that should lessen his pain. It is the cricket public who will really suffer. With Ryder's three month absence, Peter Fulton or Lou Vincent may come back, and that is a pain far worse than putting your hand through a window.

So far unsubstantiated reports have stated that Darren Lehmann and Shane Warne have gone over to set the boy straight. Jesse's parents were overheard to say, "that's all he needs".

March 2 In bed with Jacques Kallis

In March the cricket world got a little boring, so I started my own 'in bed with' series. It started with everyone's favourite love god.

CAUTION: This post contains satirically explicit sex scenes involving South Africans. If you are under 18, a prude, a religious type, or South African you should probably walk away now.

The guys over at sportsfreak.co.nz pointed me towards Kallis' extraordinary innings against the Bangladeshi kittens. 39 off 120 balls with no boundaries. This coming after the record opening partnership, which shall never be written about here. This got me thinking about how Jacques likes to have sex. I know it's a disgusting thought, but try and hold your up-chuck until the end.

Jacques comes home from a well-constructed 120 off 332 balls against New Zealand, and he says "I want to make love". You know the drill. Run him a bath. Not too hot, not too cold. You will play his favourite ocean sounds while in the bath. In the bedroom the lighting must be just right, 18 candles, they all have their positions, and cannot be moved. The music is always Kenny G, preferably Breathless, or The Moment. Following this is the maintenance session; you will thoroughly clean, wax and pluck every part of you. Jacques doesn't like grass on the wicket.

Then you must quickly log on to the internet and check out his average. You will then go into the bathroom and dry him off, all the while you will be telling him how sexy he is, how adored he is by the public, how every man wants to be him. Topics that cannot be broached: his ever widening girth, the bald spot, or the fact that no one really likes him.

This shall be followed by a slow passionless kiss, the sort of kiss that makes your toes uncurl. This kiss should go for 20 minutes. No pauses are allowed. Then the lovemaking can proceed. You will disrobe privately and quickly enter under the covers and lay naked on the bed in what is known as the starfish pose.

Jacques will then enter the bed, still under the covers and position him self on top of you, being careful not to touch you in any erotic way. He will then enter your vagina with his penis, because kiddies, that is how mummy and daddy have sex with their neighbours. At this point, you will be reasonably happy. But unfortunately, Jacques then very slowly and deliberately moves in and out, without ever going to far in, or too far out, for the next four hours.

He never once changes angle, position, speed, technique, or depth. Just a slow and steady semi-penetration until he is happy with the results, and he squeezes out a drop of Kallis juice. Never more than a drop.

Afterwards you will be required to whisper ever so sweetly 57.54 into his ear. You shouldn't be out of breath, so this should be easy to do. Then you must get Jacques' eye-mask, his ear plugs, his scented candles and leave him alone in the master bedroom to get his beauty sleep.

March 4 - Dear Jimmy

This one was written as Australia were struggling in their second final against India in the last ever triangular one day series in Australia. Jimmy Hopes was at the crease at the time.

Congratulations on a beautifully crafted innings, well, so far. I have oft compared thee to an Ian Harvey. That was wrong of me; you are much much more than Ian. You are sunshine on a cloudy day. You are the lost bourbon bottle that is found after the missus leaves. You are so wonderful, to me. Yet you grace life with a forehead so low your eyebrows get nervous.

Jimmy let me count the ways you entertain me. Slower balls. Low forehead. Wacky dismissals. Quicker-than-it-looks bowling. Catfish. General disregard for how you look on the cricket field. Drunken cowboy batting.

Even your name Jimmy, Hopes. It's not Jimmy does, or Jimmy tries, its Jimmy Hopes, and as we all know, they spring eternal.

With you at the crease our victory is practically assured. Sure we don't deserve to win, but since when has that stopped us.

Eternally yours.
(Uncle) J Rod

March 7 - The unwritten memo

More on the saga that was Australia's non-tour of Pakistan. Got called a fucking moron, socialist and artist on this one in the comments, good times.

Dear PCB,

Regretfully we have decided, about four months ago, that regardless of what happens from now on, the Australian team will not be able to tour Pakistan. I would like to apologise to the Pakistani Cricket Board on behalf of Cricket Australia. The main reason is we scheduled really badly. We have already cancelled the Bangladesh tour of Oz, "because of the Olympics", can you believe people bought that shit?

The truth is a tour of Pakistan and playing Bangladesh might tire our players and therefore we will make less money off them, so that cannot happen. We obviously will make our decision as late as possible. To the media we will state "safety concerns". People will assume we mean we are shit-scared of terrorists.

People will accept that, as people are trained in Australia to be afraid of Muslims, and all Muslims are terrorists - except you guys of course. We will schedule a tour soon, but we may cancel that to cash in on some One Dayers in India. Perhaps if Pepsi got involved we'd tour more often.

Cheers,
Cricket Australia Administracrat

March 10 - Steve's expensive balls

During England's tour of New Zealand Steve Harmison sort of lost the plot. He then said he was searching for the million dollar ball.

Steve Harmison is searching for the million dollar ball. Sounds like a reality show for the search for the perfect porn star. Harmison is odd.

This is not a new revelation. If he were born in a country with a consistently good cricket team that had a plethora of talented bowlers, he would probably not be playing international cricket. Unfortunately these things do not exist in England.

They know he is a problem child, they know he is unpredictable, but deep down they know that if he were up and firing, he could be anything. But potential is an uglier word than monogamy. Steve is now either working his way towards an IPL contract, or he is trying to find the solid copper peanut inside his head.

Drastic action needs to be taken with him. Without big brother Freddie Flintoff around, he's a goat without its herder. I suggest he forgets about this tour of New Zealand, hops on a boat for Mexico, goes out to the desert and takes a hat full of peyote.

Then he can run naked with the coyotes, play football with the locals and drink Cervasa with a pretty little senorita. Then, when his mind is somewhat closer to normal he can decide whether international cricket is a beast he wishes to slay, or whether he will go to the IPL and collect his superannuation early.

March 15 - NSWales bleed gold coins

Victoria was to take on New South Wales for the Shield title. Due to Australia's decision not to go to Pakistan, all of NSWales Australian players were free for the game. Thus meaning that Victoria had to take on Australia to win. This was from stumps at day one.

A great football coach one used a great quote from a great film made by a great action star about a great alien when he said "if it bleeds, we can kill it".

In India this Victorian side is worth a bit of IPL cash. In Australia you get a Victorian player with a Happy Meal. So the fact that they got out the Australian opening batsmen, the number four, and the next wicketkeeper on the first day was a big deal.

They also got the state player of the year out. Made Brett Lee look silly and had the mighty Speed Blitz Blues at 8 for 266 at stumps. Generally you can tell on the first day what sort of final you are going to get. If the home side win the toss and are 3 for 350 on the first day, then it's going to be shocking. This is a match.

According to Phil Jacques the day's honours were even. What a massive load of bullshit. NSWales came in with two ways of winning the title, Victoria had one, on stumps of day one we now know that a draw is out of the picture, and NSWales are not the golden gods the media made them out to be.

Victoria are not out of the woods yet. Even if they do bowl NSWales out cheaply, they still have to face Lee, who will be angry at his treatment from Siddle, Bracken, who will be confused by a red ball, Clark, who will be glad Quiney is not playing, and MacGill, who is playing for wine money.

It will not be easy, but this was Victoria's day. NSWales had a flat pitch, and it took good bowling from all three quicks to get into this position. The ball did reverse, but no non-Pakistani team can make the ball reverse better than the Vics, without mints.

The good news is, Bryce did not have to bowl great today for Victoria to be in a good position. He got the prized scalp of his bunny (ahum) the Krab Katich, but all in all he did not look that bad.

Now all the Vics need is a hundred by one of the main three and anything could happen. Former potential future PM averages over 80 against NSWales. Bring on day two, the paupers are enjoying taking on the millionaires.

March 18 - Don't kill Charl

Andre Nel was left out of South Africa's squad to India so they could fill their quota with another coloured player, Charl Langeveldt.

Charl Langeveldt has opted out of the tour to India. Because "the controversy over the selection of the squad so upset him he feels he won't be in the right frame of mind for the matches". Charl is trying to tell us that his selection due to the quota system is the reason he is not touring. Don't give us that nonsense Charl. Big Andre got to you. It's obviously partly my fault.

I did call for him to kill you, but at the time I thought it was justified, and plus it was in my podcast, so that doesn't count. I may have got that call wrong. It's just that you really bore us Charl, and I thought if Andre killed you he might get reinstated. You can see the logic in that, surely. Your death, for the greater good of the cricket watching public.

Now you have quit the tour, and have presumably gone into hiding on the same island as Hansie Cronje. I do apologise, almost sincerely, but now I will do even better: I will retract the cricket fatwa I imposed on you.

Andre, for fuck's sake don't kill the man. I have bigger plans for you anyway. Your cricket career is obviously over, so why not look into a bit of administracrat restructuring. You know the people who are calling for this quota, so find them and destroy them. Use your evil powers for good, Andre. Then when you are finished with the quota loving administracrats, you and I will take over the world.

Like we have always planned. Now be gone Andre, your master needs his rest.

March 19 - Finally

Victoria lose to New South Wales/Australia.

Is it over? Can I return to normal programming? My boys have been humbled. There is a passage from V for Vendetta that sums up how I felt before the game.

Dominic: "What do you think will happen?"
Finch: "What usually happens when people without guns stand up to people *with* guns?"

Victoria has a very good team, but not a great team. NSWales has an armoury. The pain of the situation is the false hope that you build up.

March 20 - The Easter Krab

I would like to say that some of the Australian greats of yesteryear think Simon Katich should be in the Australian side. Steve Waugh was heard to mumble "Simon Katich should be playing for Australia". But importantly he didn't say, "in cricket". Allan Border said he can do no more. I agree he can do no more, he is a krab, and krabs can only do so much.

Katich is an enigma, because if you had a shoe big enough you would crush him. And you would be right to do so. There must be something wrong with me, as all the experts see this man as someone who has restructured his game and is ready for Test cricket.

I see him as the same useless motherfucker who krabbed his way across the crease and cost us an Ashes and generally made my life miserable. Even when he made more runs than Moses this year, I still just saw the same Krab with no talent pissing me off.

Maybe there is something wrong with me. I doubt it, it's probably Katich's fault. But there is an important point to the story on Katich. Like Katich, Jesus was crucified. Jesus because he was too handsome and white to be from the Middle East, and Katich because he couldn't make any runs.

Then they were forgotten about. People got on with their lives, and then one day some smartarse checks behind a stone and Jesus was resurrected, ie his body was missing. It's similar for Katich, most of us thought we had killed the fucker and then someone one checks the scores for New South Wales, and suddenly his career was resurrected, ie, his previous shit form was forgotten.

So all I ask of you is this Good Friday is to eat a steak, and eat a krab, let's keep our long weekend resurrection-free.

March 21 - Celebrate The World Hates Graeme Day

It's some sort of Equinox. I don't really understand or care about this, but some commenters to this site seemed to think this was a sign of global unity. Who am I to argue?

But then they went further and said that the real sign of global unity is the fact everyone in the world hates Graeme Smith. I would like to believe this is true, but alas, not everyone knows Graeme Smith in the world, which is probably the only reason more people don't hate him. But if they did…….

America could hate him for out-arroganting its Olympic men's basketball team. Iran would hate him for the amount of times he comes out and says things that embarrass his people. Playground bullies would hate him, as he gives bullies a bad name. Any talented person who is poor would hate him, because he is untalented and rich. The Raelians would hate him because he does not understand that cloning and giving the Raelians headquarters in Jerusalem are the only way to salvation. Canadians would hate him, because he would remind them of Americans. Nice guys who can't get laid would hate him, because he gets laid, and is far from nice. Pets would hate him, because they would feel nervous around him. Lebanese goat herders would hate him, because as we know he hates goats.

However there are some people who may like him.

The Germaine Greer for President Society would love him, because he proves everything they have been saying for some time. Those Mongolian matriarchal women would love him, because he proves matriarchy is a viable option. The Lesbian Coalition of Turkey would love him, because he would convert new members. South Africans would love him, because they don't know any better.

Today let us celebrate the first ever The World Hates Graeme Day. You can do this by beating up your neighbour's kid, telling your friends you're better than them, or struggling for dates.

March 21 - Who is Tim Southee?

New Zealand picked a bowler from their Under 19 side to play England.

Is he a man with forefathers who liked vowels? Is he the Richard Hadlee who is not a cunt we have all been waiting for? Is he ready to break down a lot and leave for India like only a true New Zealander can? Or is he the Danny Morrison clone we have all been hoping never comes back?

I don't know, and until he takes wickets, I probably don't care. But young bowlers are exciting, even the New Zealander ones. He was recently named the best Under 19 cricketer in the world, or thereabouts. His credentials involve one Twenty20 game, and yet because he is not a drunken fat slogger, we have heard only so much about him. Perhaps if he slices his hand open in a bar, gets caught with weed, or gives a press conference about his sexuality we will care about him. New Zealanders never really get a lot of press.

Shane Bond was a demon from hell, and yet, his defection got more headlines than the 21 times he tore Australia's heart out and ate it. If Brendon McCullum were English they would dedicate monuments to him, knight him, find him a popstar girlfriend and ruin him in the space of two months. What about the Perfect Boyfriend Jacob Oram, a man so grand that if he were Sri Lankan he would be given Colombo? Of course if Lou Vincent were Australian, we would disown him and send him to some lesser country and let him play for them.

New Zealand is still a Test-playing nation; England found that out the hard way. That was just after South Africa all but proved they weren't one. But they are still the number three ranked One Day side in the world, and I'm sure if you search long and hard enough someone will care about that fact.

They aren't even as rubbish as I and everyone else in the cricket world is saying. That doesn't mean that anyone gives a shit about Tim Southee. Yet.

March 21 - How will India ruin Ishant Sharma

During India's tour of Australia, Ishant Sharma had impressed me more than any other young bowler in a long time.

I think Ishant Sharma is the most exciting young bowling prospect since Waqar Younis, assuming Waqar Younis was ever young. But he is Indian, and a real fast bowler, so you would have to assume that somewhere along the line he will fade away or lose form. Let's look at the potential ways.

His Adam's apple is actually an alien, sent from the planet Klaatu, and is intent on killing us all.
Some Bollywood producer (aka Indian mafia dude) gets him a gig on the Indian remake of Irreversible starring Aishwarya Rai, but he takes his method acting too far and in the

rape scene he slams her head into the subway floor, killing her instantly, and is lynched by horny teens everywhere.
He listens to Navjot Sidhu and Bishen Bedi for 20 minutes and his head explodes.
He gets given an English passport.
He gets caught in a lift with Sunil Gavaskar who rages about how all Australians are arseholes for two minutes and his Adam's apple inverts and chokes him from within.
Playgirl magazine offer him a billion dollars to do a naked centrefold. Indians are outraged, as his Adam's apple is airbrushed out.
Tania Zaetta meets him in a bar, and they have a torrid lust affair in which Ishant falls madly in love with her and follows her to Sydney and lives out his days as Mr Zaetta.
He shaves for the first time, but being that he is so awkward he accidentally cuts his own throat and kills himself.
Inspired by his love of Jason Gillespie he grows a ponytail and starts breaking down. Bored with cricket, women and millions of dollars he starts practicing Auto Erotic Asphyxiation. His first time ends in heartbreak (insert Adam's apple joke here).
He remembers he is Indian and starts bowling left arm orthodox or straight breaks.
The Indian government give him Bangladesh as payment for being so good, which starts a war with Pakistan, which results in America bombing the whole region. Ishant dies while tying to save a whole village of cricket academy students whose rich parents couldn't make it in time.
Me and Andre take over the world and we abduct him from India and make him play for Jrodre, the new world super power.
Pakistan get bored and fire nuclear missiles at India, thus ending his career, and the lives of countless others. Sunil Gavaskar survives.
He is raped and killed by a pack of super monkeys who are trained and controlled by Navjot Sidhu.
Everyone in India tells him he is God's gift to fast bowling until he becomes Shoaib Ahktar.
He joins the circus.

March 22 - KP & I

England's tour of New Zealand was still in progress, and Kevin Pietersen started making runs again.

I think I have KP worked out. This means one of two things; I too am a pretentious wanker who can annoy at first glance, or, somehow through my deep analysis of South Africans I have discovered what makes them tick. I'm going with the former.

Let's look at what we know about KP. In South Africa he was generally ignored and quotaed against, whilst he thought everyone should talk about him, praise him and lick the grey sticky bits from outta his toes. Goes to England, and kicks arse like a German heavy metal band.

Finally gets into the One Day side, plays his old country and treats them like a cheating husband caught on an anniversary with an uncomfortable looking goat. Then everyone says, "well KP, you're a slogger, and your hairstyle makes us think of Vanilla Ice, so we don't think we can pick you". He responds by putting Australia over his knee and giving them the biggest non-Lara spanking in a long time.

Then while people are still doubting his technique, he plays across the line too much, he charges too much, he is way too confident to play for England too much, he smotes his way around the world. What follows next is acceptance, is admiration, and is why can't we have a KP?

Which makes him think the world actually likes him, and a form slump follows. You see, KP needs to be hated; it is the very core of the man. What else could explain the hairdo, the friendship with Warney, the country of birth and the constant unnecessary charging of bowlers.

It's either he needs to be hated, or he has a little wiener. What has happened recently is that the press has finally started covering his form slump, which was one that Graeme Smith or Mark Taylor would be proud of. Llike a washed up rock star with a sampled track on the radio, KP dusted off his tight pants and made his way back to the stage.

His innings (129 out of a total of 253), which further illustrates how much better he is than anyone born in England, was the innings of a true Test-type Test-playing Test-understanding batsman.

Who knew? But now how does England keep him perennially thinking that his spot is in jeopardy and that no one likes him? Actually scratch that, if anyone can do it, the English press can.

They can turn a previously well-structured man into Steve Harmison. Although with Steve the well-structured bit is probably not true.

March 26 - Monty leads the day, Southee is the shizzle

Logically, on the day England win their first Test series is three years (that's not true, is it), I should be talking about Monty Panesar and his six wickets for 344 runs (also probably not accurate). But Monty has burned me before. When he was first picked I was assured he was humorous in the field, and while he is chuckle-worthy, he is no Tufnell.

Then I was told he just plainly couldn't bat. He's no Brett Lee but he makes Chris Martin look like a proper number 11. Also I was told he could bowl. So far, his career average is 32; it's not horrible, but it's not Portmanesque either. Instead I'm going to talk about Timothy Grant Southee, who might be more exciting than this entire series put together.

A five wicket haul in the first dig, a 77* off 40 in his last at bat. Not bad for a kid who is practically a foetus. He is only a hundred days younger than Ishant Sharma, but Sharma, while looking good in his first few tests, did not have the impact of Southee from the get-go.

Sharma's first five wicket haul was his second Test, where he slapped around a shoddy Pakistani tail. Southee destroyed England's top order first time at the crease. Plus Southee does not have an alien growing out of his throat. Take that Ishant.

Tim is unlucky. A five wicket haul and a 70 gets you seven figures in India, Sir Ian Botham comparisons in England, and in Australia he wouldn't be playing because he is a bowler and under 25.

Where to now for this youngster? Will he become the cricketer that drags New Zealand back into real Test playing status? Will he make a lot of dollars when he retires from the national side for personal reasons to play in the ICL? Or will he become a statistical footnote in the slow decline of modern culture?

Exactly.

March 27 - Me vs The Wisden Cricketer, this time it's intimate

I was encouraged, by The Wisden Cricketer (shameless publicity hounds that they are) to start a campaign to get myself into their best of the blogs section, so I did.

I am Australian. So it is in my blood to be a competitive bastard. And I am, oh how I am. Now that kingcricket.co.uk has been in Wisden as Blog of the Month, I am thinking that I should be too. Obviously the extremely well hung men and women of the Wisden Cricketer may not share my view. Not yet anyway. But they will. Because you are going to help me on my new internet campaign. Send UJR (me) to The Wisden Cricketer.

Obviously now that the David Hussey petition (sign here) is being taken to the streets, Cricket With Balls needs a new internet goal, and that goal is Wisden. Or in the words of Vince Vaughn, "Wisden Baby Wisden".

So if you think I should be put in The Wisden Cricketer, please comment below. If you think I shouldn't be put in The Wisden Cricketer please comment below. If you think that King Kong is a lesbian please comment below.

So The Wisden Cricketer, I hope you're ready for a fight, and in the words of Lee Marvin, "I know you're horny Fritz, but you got bad breath".

March 28 - Jesus, Moses, Madonna, and Paris Hilton are out, Sehwag is in

This post represents the birth of Sehwagology. The cricket world's first unifying religion. Sehwag had just made a triple century against the South Africans.

I'm not an expert on global politics, free markets, terrorism, or why people watch reality TV. But I do know that all these things pale into insignificance when compared to Virender Sehwag's innings. Natalie Portman turns ugly. George Clooney loses charm. Dubya Bush makes sense. Britney Spears puts knickers on. And Tony Greig is palatable after this innings.

It is the sort of innings that could turn Amelie Mauresmo straight and keep Warnie's pee pee in his pants. If it were a hot woman, you could not only not score with it, but if you were in the same room, your tool would melt. It could start and end wars. Upon viewing it aliens would be afraid to invade. If you had the Colt 45 cocked and pointed at your mouth you would put it down and pick up a cricket bat.

Sehwag batted so well the earth started spinning in other directions. No one has been this unkind to the saffas since Muhammad Ali turned his back on a young Barry Richards. When the Africans were killed by tribes of Zulus it was nowhere near this brutal. Batting at the other end was not a spectator sport, but a voyeuristic thrill ride through the realms of batting thought beyond those of mere mortals.

It was so good, there was a good 15 seconds when Sunil Gavaskar didn't bag white people, Bishen Bedi didn't accuse everyone of being a chucker, and Navjot Sidhu made sense.

Yoko Ono and Paul McCartney had intercourse during his third hundred. Palestinians invited Israelis around for a beer after a particular over of Ntini. Anna Nicole Smith came back from the dead to give an interview for Entertainment Tonight, during the tea interval for maximum exposure. Michael Moore went down on Dick Cheney. Nothing to do with Sehwag, just wanted to see if it was his bag.

The Spice Girls split up after a fight over who would get to sleep with Sehwag. Tom Cruise became a Sehwagologist. And you know what, so should you.

Everyone should; I'm assuming all it takes is a little Friar Tuck action, a rotund little figure, balls the size of Jupiter and a touch of owl's blood. Join Sehwagology, it's cheaper than other religions, twice as cool, and comes with its own action hero.

309 off 292, put the kids to bed woman, we have business to attend to.

March 29 - My Sehwag list

These are the things I would gladly give up or away to have been at the ground watching Sehwag yesterday.

The birth of my second child.
Keira Knightley (not Natalie) offering herself to me.

Victoria winning the Sheffield Shield at the MCG, with Nice Bryce taking the last wicket of Simon Katich.
A swingers party where the Dixie Chicks were the only other guests.
The chance to direct Phillip Seymour Hoffman and Benicio Del Toro.
My left little toe.
The chance to open for Dana Lyons.
My donkey stuffed toy I won in one of those claw machines that no one ever wins in.
The chance to play for the Kolkata Knight Riders.
An afternoon chat with Richie Benaud over a glass of port.
The ability to get away with beating up Tony Greig.

April 1 - Beau Casson selects the right state

Australia pick their squad for the West Indies, and I disagree slightly on the spin bowling selections.

Oh I'm fucking pissed off right now. Beau fucking Casson. Fucking New South Wales does it again. Who the fuck is Beau Casson you may ask. Well he was a Western Australian who got snatched by New South Wales and obviously got told if he came to New South Wales all his fears of never playing for Australia would evaporate. The touring squad of the West Indies has been selected and Beau Casson's Baggy Green can be taken out of the brown paper bag.

Bryce McGain's Baggy Green remains as real as the moon landing or Pamela Anderson's breasts. According to Andrew Hilditch, chief selector of New South Wales and Australia, "we have taken the opportunity to take a young spinner and by far the best performed of these during the Australian summer has been Beau Casson". What he means is, we aren't taking Bryce McGain because he is a, too old, b, too Victorian.

Let's take the bloke who bowled on a spinner's paradise all year and still ended up with nine less wickets than McGain and with a worse average. And that doesn't even take into account the fact that Casson picked up a four wicket haul when the Vics were making a reckless play for glory on the fifth day crumbler at the SCG. That was the day Dirty Dirk smashed him around.

Of course he is the best young spinner in the country, because there simply are no others. But mid-way through the year he couldn't buy a wicket with a stolen credit card. Don't you dare mention his batting, Andrew. Someone who bats like him is not a test match all-rounder; at best he is a Hoggard/Gillespie tailender at this stage.

Suddenly the Australian selectors are worrying about the age of cricketers; suddenly they don't want the second best spinner, but the spinner who is younger. So does this mean they have changed their selection policies again? Weren't they picking the best cricketers regardless of age when Clark, Hodge and Hussey were picked? Do they have selection policies? Is there a website I can click onto that says, CA Selection Policy, download here for pdf, or click here if you want itwritten in goat's blood on your dog's corpse.

I personally had high hopes for Beau Casson when he was a youngster, but having seen him bowl some horribly benign spells this year, in person, in the very same game Bryce took five for against a better batting line up, there is simply no question who the better bowler is right now. If we choose to play two spinners in the West Indies, then the second spinner cannot be a project player, he must be a Test match strength spinner, and right now, for this tour, Bryce is the better option.

He puts pressure on batsmen, he rarely bowls bad balls, and he gets the very best batsmen out. Plus he almost single-handedly won Victoria the Ford Ranger Cup with a spell of bowling that had Bill Lawry's Pigeon looking very nervous. But I'm not biased at all.

April 3 - The Scriptures of Sehwagology

The 10 Virendments - Sehwag's Revelation in the Old Testament (Wisden).

They were given directly by Sehwag to the people of India at
Chidambaram Stadium after He had delivered them from Boredom in Chennai:

"And Sehwag spoke all these words, saying: 'I am the opening batsmen, your God…

ONE: 'You shall have no other Gods before Me, except Sachin and maybe Sunil'.
TWO: 'You shall not make for yourself a carved image in any likeness of anything that is in heaven above, or that is in the earth beneath, or that is in the water under the earth. In fact don't carve anything that is not wide outside off stump'.
THREE: 'You shall not take the name of the LORD your God in vain, so if you stub your toe, try not to say Oh Sehwag'.
FOUR: 'Remember the third day, the pitch is often at its best'.
FIVE: 'Honour your father and your mother, and your sponsors'.
SIX: 'You shall not murder, exceptions made for opening bowlers, spinners and Probots'.
SEVEN: 'You shall not commit quick singles'.
EIGHT: 'You shall not be worrying about playing and missing'.
NINE: 'You shall not bear false witness against the BCCi'.
TEN: 'You shall not covet your neighbour's house; you shall not covet your neighbour's wife, nor his male servant, nor his female servant, nor his ox, nor his donkey, but if he bowls a wide half volley hit it like it stole your donkey or ox'."

April 9 - A long beau

Australia's list of contracted players gets announced, and it's odd, but not surprisingly so.

Ok so let me get this straight. Shaun Tait gets a contract because he has depression. Ben Hilfenhaus gets a contract because he was good last year. Doug Bollinger gets a contract because he is from NSWales. But Peter Sizzle (Siddle) does not because he is Victorian. Actually that all makes sense.

Now on to the spinners. Last year there were four. Stuart MacGill who at that stage was slightly fitter and not so much a TV presenter. Brad Hogg who at that stage was still being called a spinner. Dan Cullen who at that stage was getting fewer wickets than Brad Hogg. And Cullen Bailey, who is the second highest paid club cricketer in Australian history behind another leg spinner, Abdul Qadir.

This year we have Stuart MacGill, a little older, a little rounder, and a little less interested. Beau fucking Casson, the man who has played four good games in four seasons, but moved to the right city.

And… oh that's it. Australia is only going to use these two this year. That's it.

An untried wrist spinner who couldn't buy a wicket for years, and a 37-year-old wine connoisseur with a bung knee. No place for Bryce McGain, let's check why, oh that is right, he's Victorian. The only thing that remains consistent for selectors is that NSWelsh players get picked all the time, and Victorians get the high hard one.

April 12 - Unkie J talks leggies

A small boy entered the pizza shop today and said "Hey Unkie J, I want to be a leg spinner just like you", and I said "Well I am a hybrid bubbly/club leg spinner". The little boy ran out confused. That left me worried about the state of education in our schools. Are kiddies not taught about the variants of leg spinning? Maybe some on my blog are confused also.

Leg spinning types and brief descriptions, by Unkie J.

The Aussie ripper leg spinner
Practised by Peter McIntyre, Stuart MacGill, and Shane Warne.

The main art of this leg spinner is the actual side spin imparted on the ball, which is done with a slightly rounder arm action and wrists made of steel. The objective is to spin the ball sideways on glass whilst maintaining a fairly consistent length and line. In lesser hands it can go horribly wrong. In the hands of a master, it can be combined with subtler straighter balls and gentle over spin to keep the batsman guessing. Mostly a leg stump line, can be less effective against a cack hander.

Signature move: the ball that spins past the outside edge.

The Bubbly Pakistani leg spinner
Practised by Mushtaq Ahmed and Abdul Qadir.

This is leg spin with a touch of aerobics. It requires lots of hopping, arm whipping and an off stump line. This is the one form of leg spin that best encapsulates everything there is about leg spinning, as all deliveries are available from a straighter arm action whilst still spinning the ball. The objective is to trick the batsmen with a variant of balls so devilishly devised that he regularly plays for a ball that spins one way while it spins the other way. Because the ball spins both ways it is effective against all batsmen, but the off stump line means a good length is very important.

Signature move: the wrong'un that cuts the batsman in two halves.

The absurdist straight breaker
Practised by Tiger Bill O'Reilly, Anil Kumble, Shahid Afridi, Chris Harris, Cameron White, and Piyush Chawla.

This is leg spin without the leg spin. It is deception of the highest order. It is also almost impossible to make a living on. You must have the ability to sell the spin, while delivering the straight one. You can bowl any delivery you want with this style, but it doesn't really matter, because you won't be spinning the ball anyway, but if you are good at it, you will be aggressively accurate and steady like a train. The objective is to penetrate the mind of the batsmen through repetition and absurdity.

Signature move: the straight one.

The club leg spinner
Practised by Richie Benaud, Bryce McGain, and every West Indian leg spinner ever.

Not a huge spinner of the ball, has variation but mostly works on the fact that if they can land every leg spinner in the same place for a day, wickets will come. The arm action is usually somewhere between straight arm and round arm, and this particular style comes in many wonderfully different actions. The objective is to beat the batsman with subtle flight, spin and speed changes.

Signature move: the batsman losing patience and swinging across the line, but hitting it straight up in the air.

The Paul Adams leg spinner
Practised by Paul Adams, and me in the backyard until I hurt my back.

Was once described as a frog in a blender. I like to think of it as a midget, wearing a bunny suit, trying to fling its head at you with a shoulder jerk so savage that it could kill the average ostrich. The objective seems to be not to fling your head at the batsman, but to make him think you are while you get him with your badly disguised wrong one.

Signature move: unknown.

April 14 - The new Jack Iverson

Ajantha Mendis stormed onto the international scene (well as much as you can if you aren't from England, Australia or India) by taking apart the West Indies. I called for calm; no one listened.

I have decided to take a severe disliking to Ajantha Mendis. Not hatred, just yet. For the three of you that haven't heard, he is the new wonder spinner, part Saqlain Mushtaq, part Shane Warne, part John Gleeson and a whole lotta Jack Iverson. Usually the idea of a spinner who can bowl wrong 'uns, flippers, doosras and everything in between would have me gooey in the nether regions.

But everyone has already proclaimed this guy the messiah of spin bowling. Not because he can bowl well but because he can bowl so many different deliveries. Don't get me wrong, I don't blame the kid, I blame the media. Everyone else does, don't they Shaun Tait?

So far he has played two games, and he is already the future of spin bowling. John Gleeson would be rolling over in his grave, if he were dead. We don't really know if he can bowl or not; what we know is he has the ability to bowl six or seven different types of deliveries. So do I. I can bowl every delivery on his list except for the doosra.

None of them well. Some of them, like the flipper, spectacularly bad. The ability to bowl seven different deliveries doesn't ensure your future as a Test cricketer. Bowling two deliveries really fucking fantastically is usually what does it.

I really do hope this guy is the real deal. If not, a lot of people who aren't me will look like complete tools.

April 17 - My IPL thoughts

I thought on this semi-momentous day, I'd give you some of my thoughts on the IPL.

I don't like the name: sounds like a name for accountancy firm, and Indian Premier League is much better yet greatly ignored. I do hope Twenty20 games will eventually out-strip One Day games, but it's the club format that I don't like. Australian soccer players have all sorts of trouble getting their clubs to ok them to play for their country, and there are way more international cricket games than soccer friendlies.

In a country where people starve I think that this sort of opulence is obscene. The only reason any Indian should spend money on Ashwell Prince is so he can be carved up and served at dinnertime to the indignant. Ricky Ponting and Future PM David Hussey have to play for Sourav. I always felt sorry for the Indians who played under him, but now Australians are doing it, and more importantly David Hussey. It's shocking.

Victorians are finally getting their dues in the IPL: shunned at home, but lauded abroad, like Nick Cave and Jason Donovan. The names of the teams, Knight Riders, some sort of medieval sexual name; Super Kings, much better than usual kings. And why are all the teams monarchists, where are the republican teams?

Cheerleaders. I've never got them. I know I'm a pervert, but I get no thrill from watching cheerleaders. Either get naked and have an orgy, or put your clothes on and sit down. Bollywood stars: why?

Domestic cricketers are finally getting paid what they are owed. For too long if you weren't in the top 15 players in your country you were paid a similar wage to a plumber.

The length of the tournament: good luck keeping people interested for 42 days.

I wish it well, mostly.

April 20 – IPL improvements

In this post I mentioned using lasers on players, which then happened during an international Twenty20 game in Brisbane. I am learning how to deal with my tremendous influence.

Twenty20 is still not perfect. In 2007 I wrote about possible improvements for Twenty20 cricket. These were based on the Australian model. Now these are my improvements for the Indian model.

As every team seems to have one celebrity owner, why not do something more with them than just cut to them 83 times per match. At the interval they should have to fight each other to the death. Most of them are Bollywood stars anyway, and there is plenty more where that came from.

Aamir Sohail and Greg Chappell should be allowed to do five minutes of stand up comedy before each game, to the death.

Since all the cheerleaders had to be flown in, why not replace them with actual porn stars, no need for flirty failed dancers. Just get porn stars in, they can be clothed during the game.

The opening ceremony had laser shows; why not allow two young kids to have lasers during the game, and point them at whoever they feel the need to temporarily blind.

No matter what the score is, for the last over 19 runs is needed. That way we may get to combine the slogging with close finishes.

Every team should have one player who goes out on the field in traditional Sikh clothing. Sword included, and if they deem it necessary they can cut off the hand of a team-mate who continually fields badly.

Players should be escorted out onto the ground with a lady on each arm, or a man if they swing that way.

If the cheerleaders are to be kept, they should be allowed to play, possibly instead of Ganguly.

Batting orders should be reversed at the discretion of the first drunken fan who is evicted. If none are evicted, the last person evicted from the MCG should make decisions.

Robert Mugabe should take over a team, and then take over the whole league and start killing the other celebrity owners, while starving the players.

Mascots should play a game against each other, to the death.

Finally we need some sort of spiritual aspect: let's get that young girl with the two faces down, and sit her in the middle of the ground during the break. And then let her bite the two players she hates the most.

That is my kind of league.

April 22 - Eyelids takes over Notts

This is the Nostradamus of cricket posts, even if it was satirical. Introducing Darren "Eyelids" Pattinson.

I couldn't believe my eyes (no need for that pun). Darren Pattinson, also known as Eyelids, is strutting his stuff for Nottinghamshire, which is not a side in the IPL. Eyelids was born in the UK, but was brought up in Victoria, hence why he is a shit hot fast bowler. His nickname Eyelids comes from his approach to the wicket where his eyelids seem to flap around a lot and it often looks as if he is coming in to bowl with his eyes closed.

He was mentioned to Notts by none other than the Future PM himself, David Hussey. For the Notts faithful who visit this site, which would be thousands, I will illuminate Eyelids for you. He is a chesty front on sort of bowler, who can bowl into the 140s down breeze on a windy day and moves the ball around a bit. He doesn't look like a superstar, but the man gets wickets quite often, perhaps by making the batsman confused at the man running in with his eyes shut.

His first game ended with eight wickets against Kent, who from memory have no players of any real skill, but he did get out Robert Key, who I think once might have played for England. Eyelids also made a stoic 33-odd, so this is a very good start for the man, who I presume will play for England within the next four months.

Oh and Eyelids has a younger brother as well, who is a bowling clone of Eyelids, who has really big wraps on him and who has already played for the Australian under-whatever side, so probably can't play for England. Such a shame, as from all reports, the kid is a super freak.

April 26 - Howlin' bawler

During the IPL, Harbhajan Singh slapped Sreesanth, and the world laughed.

Men can cry. Michael Jordan has cried. George W Bush has cried. Even Hilary Clinton has cried. In this day and age, men crying isn't held to be as wimpy as it once was. People now even see men crying as way more acceptable than women crying. The world has changed.

But two Indian men, one feminine enough to slap another man, another feminine enough to cry about it, are testing the world's new found acceptance of male bawling. Sreesanth cried because a man slapped him. Is there any coming back from that?

It was only days ago I talked about how cool he was, via blog and podcast. The whole angry man fast bowler thing was back; he was abusing people and being a giant arse-clown, just how I like it. Now he is crying after Harbhajan Singh, of all people, slapped him.

This is how I would have expected this story to go.
"Harbhajan Singh is in critical condition in Mumbai Indian hospital today, after an incident with his Indian team-mate and IPL sparring partner Sreesanth. Harbhajan Singh allegedly slapped Sreesanth, before Sreesanth slammed his head into a wall an unknown number of times, leaving Harbhajan Singh severely injured. No charges have been laid, but Sreesanth is helping police with their enquires".

I would not have expected this. "Harbhajan slaps Sreesanth, who then cries in the corner naked and wet, waiting for his mother to bring over his favourite blanky".

April 26 - Everybody hurts, Sreesanth

Everyone is laughing at Sreesanth. Justifiably. But fast bowlers are an emotional dichotomy.

Shaun Tait wants to rip heads off, but the stress of not doing so makes him sad.
Brett Lee wants to be a nice guy, but every now and then he forgets and bowls beamers.
Dale Steyn is South African.
Steve Harmison is part animal, part machine. Problem is, it's a guinea pig and an electric tie organiser.
Shane Bond is made of ice cream; chocolate chip.
And Andre Nel cried when he hit Allan Donald in a domestic game.

That's right. Andre Nel, Sreesanth's sick adopted brother, has also cried on the cricket field. Sure his was because he smashed his idol in the face with an angry bouncer, not because a little girly man slapped him, but a cry is a cry.

Perhaps mentalist fast bowlers aren't as tough as we always thought they were.

Maybe Thommo cries every time he mispronounces Glenn McGrath's name. Chances are Demon Fred Spofforth got upset every time he didn't get a hat trick. Fiery Fred Trueman may have reached for the tissue when the selectors overlooked him for a more "gentlemanly" chap. Craig McDermott probably bawls every time he misplaces his video camera. Perhaps even the mighty Wes Hall cried when he broke Colin Cowdrey's arm.

I guess fast bowlers do have feelings. Who knew?

May 3 - If it wasn't for arsonists, would we have the Ashes?

Mark Vermeulen is a little-known Zimbabwean player who set fire to the Zimbabwean Cricket Academy. But he was cleared on grounds of mental illness, sustained from a knock to the head from Irfan Pathan.

One of my vigilant readers sent me an email saying, "Not sure if you'd caught up on the fact that Mark Vemeulen is considering a comeback. Apparently he just wants a couple of matches..." Thanks LG.

This caught my eye for two reasons. One, he made a great arson related pun. And two, because it is true. The man who was deemed too mentally ill to commit arson wants to come back to international cricket. Of course he hasn't mentioned that the reason he left international cricket was that Irfan Pathan hit him with a cream pie.

But should we let mentally ill people play cricket? It's an interesting question, so I posed it to Andre Nel. He head-butted me.

So I asked Sreesanth, but he ran away, stripped down naked and began flicking away imaginary rats.

I got hold of Michael Clarke, who said "narcissism is not a mental illness you know, it's a personality disorder".

From there I contacted Freddie Flintoff, but he couldn't hear me over the clanking of his beer bottles in his hyperbaric chamber.

I talked to Shoaib, he seemed to really warm to me, I spoke to him for about ten minutes, before he turned to his minder and said "I don't think this guy has any coke".

After all that I got hold of Jesse Ryder who said "Fucked if I know mate, can you hold that Tequila for me, my hand is fuckin' killing me".

May 4 - You said I was your cousin

Steve Harmison will consider quitting cricket if he is not selected for England again. I think I speak for a lot of cricket fans the world over when I say; fuck off. No really, just fuck off. Don't consider, just do it already.

There are a bunch of English bowlers who would play domestic cricket for 15 years just for the chance to play for England. How hard is it to carry your own bags and take wickets domestically? Ottis Gibson did it for fuck's sake. And what is he, like 2000 years old? Steve Harmison is finished.

He seems to spend more time saying odd things to the press than actually working on his game. His one unplayable ball followed by three wides is no longer tolerated. Even he is not interested: "I am 29 now and if I felt my England career was over I would be tempted to say I want to do something different with my life".

But what would you do Harmy?

Fast bowling is the only thing you look like you can do, and you have never really mastered it.

However, given that Harmy has entertained me many times, often unintentionally, I thought I'd help out.

Jobs for Harmy.

Bouncer at a club; you are big and ugly enough.
Wax statue of yourself at Madame Tussauds; you can go in the 2005 exhibition.
Press Secretary for George W Bush.
Pakistani dictator; being erratic is encouraged.
You could play Lennie Small from Of Mice and Men in high school productions across England.

Freddie Flintoff will make a good George when he works out his body was not made for non-contact sport.

May 4 - Warne, ahoy hoy

With Warne's success as captain of the Rajasthan Royals in the IPL, the familiar calls about his captaincy were brought back up.

Ian Chappell is pushing a familiar wagon. Warne as captain. Once Ian gets a woody over a girl, it doesn't matter if she becomes a nun, the man still talks about it about what he thinks it would have been like to bonk her for the next 30 years. It's almost as if he doesn't think repetition is annoying. It's almost as if he doesn't think repetition is annoying. It's almost as if he doesn't think repetition is annoying.

This is one of those occasions where he is right. Warne would have been a captain and a half. But did he have to bag all the other boring Victorian captains while doing so? Our last three captains have been pretty adventurous and attacking, it was just the hundred years before that they were a bit boring. Being from Melbourne I probably haven't seen Warne captain as much as say someone from his home town of Hampshire has, but I have seen enough.

The first time I saw Warne captain was for Australia in a One Day series against England and Sri Lanka. The Australian team was good, but it still had some duds in it. Brendon Julian, Shane Lee and Adam Dale to be exact. Australia won ten of the 11 games in that series. And Warne's captaining was the reason.

The main thing I remember about that series was that when batsmen were hitting balls down to third man for easy singles, he would plug the gap with a third or fourth slip and let them roll the dice, even if it was in the 47th over. Also like Rajasthan now, he had them up and excited. They thought they could win every game, no matter what happened. They were a cohesive well-oiled machine that played more like an Aussie Rules team than a cricket team.

Then Steve Waugh came back, and he captained his way. Which, while being extremely effective in Tests, wasn't really suited to One Day cricket, and Australia only won the 1999 World Cup because Warne, McGrath and Steve were too good when it mattered. The actual team performed terribly in that World Cup.

For Victoria, the few times I saw him captain them, his tactics were impressive, but what was most impressive was the way he got players to lift for him. Ian Harvey was a good player for Victoria, but when he played under Warne, he was Freakin' Freddie Flintoff. Darren Berry seemed to only be able to bat when Warne was around. And a bunch of journeymen state players stepped up under him time and time again.

The only downside I have noticed over the years is that Warne doesn't bowl quite as well as captain, but Warne at 90 per cent is usually enough. What you are now seeing from the Victorian Royals is a combination of that. Tactics that are baffling the opposition. A mentality of we can win from anywhere. The team playing like a footy team, hunting in a pack. The younger players feeling inspired. The older players feeling liberated. And Warne at the helm telling everyone that he is the man.

If only he had kept his dick in his pants, like Keith Miller before him.

May 7 - Ol' Stuey

The host of Uncorked, Stuart MacGill, has decided to put aside his day job for a while to concentrate on his part time hobby, cricket. What should Australia expect from this ever-widening wrist spinner with the aloof smirk who enunciates his words correctly? He has a knee that can never be fixed. Earlier this year he played hide and seek with administracrats to film his show. He is returning from wrist surgery that usually middle-aged virginal men have. And possibly the most important thing about Stuey MacGill is that he is now happy.

So what can Australia expect of this newer old version of Stuey?

Well sooner rather than later he will celebrate a wicket like he has just gutted a pig, with a spork. His next wicket will not be celebrated at all, and he will look down at anyone who does celebrate it. At times he will bowl half trackers and full tosses; he will mix them up with the odd unplayable delivery. He will bowl a lot of balls short and wide of off stump, some of which will have pitched on the stumps.

When he bats he will miss the ball a lot, back away, scoop the ball, smile at his crapness with the stick and go out. He will run as fast as he can after balls, while being overtaken by Symonds jogging. Balls that your mother could stop will go through him from time to time. When he does stop a hard ball, he will have that look that every middle-aged dude who does something good on a reality show has. He will look angry a lot. He will look mildly amused a lot.

In general, being 37, fatter and more injured than before really won't change Stuart MacGill on the field. As he has played like an old unfit dude his whole career.

May 7 - Where in the world is Dirty Dirk Nannes?

Dirk Nannes is a favourite of Cricket With Balls, and in this post, infrequent guest poster Miriam finds out he is signed to Middlesex, but there is no explanation as to why he is not playing.

The other day, a little flyer popped into my letterbox.

MISSING: Dirty Dirk Nannes.
LAST SEEN: "Apparently, last seen boarding a plane to Japan to (not) ski ... before fattening his wallet in the UK".
APPEARANCE: Bearded.
REWARD FOR INFORMATION: a photo of Natalie Portman, autographed by Jrod, OR a photo of Jrod, autographed by Natalie, depending on gender of finder.

Well, with a reward like that, how could I not try to win? So, I began my quest to find him. I understood from my informer, Deep Throat, that he likes falling over a lot. So the first stop was a bouncy castle at a fair. However, when I described the nature of the mission in order to garner a search party from amongst my fellow detectives, they all said "bearded man frequenting funfairs on his own? Nah, this is specialist stuff luv, you wanna go up to the fifth floor for the people who do that".

Next stop was a CAMRA festival, as he is a bearded man. But when I showed them the picture, they said "Call that a beard? I've seen more convincing beards standing next to Tom Cruise". Next, I tried walking the street wearing an "I'm Looking For Dirty Dirk" t-shirt. Maybe the text was too small or something, but all I got was "right here, baby!" Over and over again. And none of these people were Dirk.

Someone asked me "well where did you leave him?". I did explain that if I knew that, he wouldn't be lost. Someone else said "you'll find him in the last place you look, you mark my words!". I did explain that this was the case with any kind of search, as people do not generally continue looking for something after they have found it. I had nearly given up hope. I'd been around the world (it seemed), but I I I, I couldn't find my Dirty Dirk. This quest was as ill-advised as Gwyneth Paltrow's pink Ralph Lauren Oscar dress.

Then I remembered that when you have lost something and can't find it, you're supposed to look in the place where you least expect to find it. So I tried Middlesex's starting XI. No joy there even. But on the way out of Lord's, in the pouring rain, I almost tripped over a huddled figure seated on the ground wrapped in a blanky. I avoided eye contact, but then he said "spare some change, miss?" and something about the rising intonation at the end of his sentence made me turn round and look, and there he was! I've never been any good at "Name That Bum", but today I'd hit the jackpot.

He said "all I wanted was a game, just a game of cricket". So I gave him a copy of International Cricket Captain 3. "Oh" he said. "Version 2 is better". I said "Dirk, Dirk, Dirk. You know what I'm going to say, don't you? Yes, that's right. Someone like you who is destitute in the street asking for a game is not in a position to express a preference as to what kind of game".

Dirty Dirk, if you're out there, come say hello. This is a safe place.

May 8 – IPL (press snooze now)

I watched 75 per cent of the first game between The Hasselhoffs (Kolkata Knight Riders) and the royal old dudes (Bangalore Royals). That remains to this point the game I have spent the most time actually watching. All the games are now fusing into to each other like episodes of Charmed. You know you saw something you liked. You know it appealed to your base instincts. You know other things happened during the episode as well, but in the end you are left with the vision of Alyssa Milano in a tight top and everything else has faded away.

The games seem over before they begin. Without the Kiwis and Aussies the league seems a little more stale. I still can't remember who is playing for who. The only time I get excited is when there is a scandal. There is a game every 15 minutes. By the time I work out there is a game on, and I turn the telly on, the contest is over. Every team has someone I like, love, hate or despise in them, so you can't even support the teams properly.

Twenty20 is a quicker form of the game, and it even got boring at 10 times the speed One Day cricket has. And I can never remember who the hell I'm supporting (checked my calendar today it's the super duper kings (Chennai Super Kings)).

Maybe the IPL isn't for me. Perhaps I should leave it for the serious cricket correspondents (wellpitched.com).

And this dude (outsidetheline.typepad.com).

From here on in, my IPL coverage shall be phoned in. If it's good enough for Robert DeNiro to do for ten years, it's good enough for me.

May 15 - IPL bombs

During the IPL bombs went off in Jaipur, home of the Rajasthan Royals.

Darren Berry is a tough bastard. He is built like a pick up truck, carrying a large round pile of hay. In all the years I saw him play for Victoria I never saw him back down to anyone. If you were dating his sister, you would make sure she broke up with you. But right at the moment he is scared, even if he calls it "uncomfortable".

Bombs have gone off in Jaipur, killing up to 80 people. If this was Pakistan, or Sri Lanka, Warne and Smith would be sipping champagne in first class, a cold beer in business for Watson and Berry. But India, like England, seems to convince people to stay, even if all logic declares otherwise.

According to some American website I checked, terrorists have killed 2,300 people in India. I am not one for trusting Americans, but if that is right, 2,300 people seems a lot to die from terrorism in one year. Pakistan lost a tour because someone assassinated someone we all know. Andrew Symonds said he was nervous about going there. Give him a cheque and he is happy to fly just over the boarder where a mere 2,300 non-famous people have been killed.

The only cricket ground in the world that has been targeted that I know of is the MCG. Players continue to travel here. As they do to London, and as they have to India. The difference now is that it is happening in the city of Jaipur, home of the Royal Warnes, and Darren Berry certainly seemed to notice: "it is terrifying. To think I was standing in the exact location the bombs went off only two days ago ... it was a couple of kilometres from the team hotel. The whole country has gone into lockdown".

I know money talks, and I know that is why Pakistan and Sri Lanka struggle to overcome their bomb blasts, but Shane Watson is a contracted Cricket Australia player. The same Cricket Australia who said Pakistan was not for them. The obvious decision is that they pull young Shane home, as he is the sort of dude who gets injured thinking about eating ice cream.

The IPL has already decided that the next game will be played in Jaipur, not shifted somewhere else, which is one of two things.

1) Arrogant we-don't-bow-down-to-terrorism crap.
2) Money talks realism.

This is going to be an interesting couple of days. *(Edit for the book: nothing happened, the IPL went on and no players went home. True story)*

May 14 – Stop moaning, start drinking

Miriam tried to help people deal with the tedium of the IPL by inventing a drinking game.

I've picked up the very slight impression that a few of you might be the teensiest bit bored of the IPL.

Some might say that a man who is bored of the IPL is bored of life. There's only one sleep [ONE SLEEP, PEOPLE!] before a Test starts, so you don't have to wait much longer for the excitement of watching two tailenders scratch out a draw on a wearing fifth day pitch, instead of all these fast-paced colourful fireworks.

Here at Cricket With Balls, though, instead of constantly moaning about how bored we are, we make our own entertainment (just like during the war), and there is one sure-fire way to liven up any boring event.

ALCOHOL!
So, here are some IPL drinking games to get you through. Don't say we never think of you.

1. Drink 1 finger for:

Everytime SRK dances.
Every six scored.
Every time DLF is mentioned.
Every time Pommie Mbwanga says "Jackers".
Every occurrence of any of the following phrases: "it's gone the distance", "it's the maximum", "that's out of the park".

For the avoidance of doubt, if all of the above happen in relation to the same shot, that's a finger for each thing.

2. Drink 2 fingers for the following sightings:

A player wears a shirt that is manifestly not his, and the cruder the attempt at covering the original owner's name and number, the better.

A dugout interview is held in a non-English speaking player's native language, with an English interviewer, but not translated.
A commentator interviews a player and confuses which side he is on.
Sachin Tendulkar.

3. Down whatever's in your glass when:

A wicket falls.
There is any mention of the orange cap.

4. Everyone in the room must drink a flaming Sambuca in the event of:

A hat-trick.
A game won by a last-ball six.

5. A special celebratory bottle of champagne is to be kept on ice and broken out if any of the following happen:

Misbah finds yet another innovative way of getting out.
Microphones pick up evidence of long-held festering grudges ("justice will get you one day Sourav").
Anyone adopts the mock slap as their wicket celebration.

If you're still bored after all that, we may have to resort to Strip IPL.

May 20 - England to win three-zip

Before New Zealand's tour of England I predicted England would win three-nil at home, the first Test was a draw that finished on the 19th of May, but I like to stick to my guns, even in a three Test series.

The English cricket team are an amazing breed of players. Batsmen who look the part, talk the talk, get the plaudits, and produce very little. Bowlers who are rejects from the Ford Modelling Agency. And wicketkeepers that come on a conveyor belt of pasty balding fumblers who can bat a bit. It's a weird mix. On top of this, about every two years England has a new saviour, someone to deliver them to the promised land. England's recent list of saviours:

Harmy, who, if he were a gladiator, would eat the lion one day, and get eaten by a mouse the next. Freddie Flintoff, the drunkard superstar who can do anything on a cricket field, if only he was regularly on them. KP was South African, but unfortunately he had to pledge his allegiance to England so many times that he is now English, and therefore not the saviour. Let us not forget Monty, who we were all assured was going to usher in a new breed of spin success for England, and now just gets in the way of a Yorkshire leggie (potential Cricket with balls' own Adil Rashid).

New Zealand are New Zealand, and no one can deny them that.

Prince Brendon is a one man wrecking crew. The Perfect Boyfriend Oram is a one man wrecking crew. And Daniel Vettori is a foreman, who operates his two one man wrecking crews. Other than that everyone is a battler. Some, like Taylor, could be one man wrecking crews, but they keep destroying themselves. Chris Martin, a man who looks so dodgy Daniel Flynn bats with his wallet in his creams, can bowl a bit, and so can former Adonis Kyle Mills. Jamie How is something, we are just not sure what at the moment.

So where does this leave this series? England maybe could have won, but they went for the draw. New Zealand could never have won, but they finished on top. England has a lot of improving to do. New Zealand are playing in their 99th percentile.

England three-zip it is; I like to stick by my guns, even when I'm shooting myself in the foot.

May 20 - Monty, you're a starfish

I had high hopes for Monty Panesar. The first reports were he could really bowl. That he could really not bat. And that he fielded like a particularly uncoordinated cerebral palsy afflicted platypus. None of these are true.

His bowling is average. It's not Ashley Giles bad, but it's not Murali good. His batting is pretty ordinary, but it's not laugh until you need to pee ordinary like Chris Martin; it's more vanilla ordinary. His fielding is pretty crap, but it's not you could watch him all day crap.

In a word he is meh. He is just another left arm tweaker from England. He doesn't really spin the ball all that much. He doesn't really instil fear into opposition batsman. He averages over 32 with the rock. He doesn't take drugs, or say odd things. He doesn't seem to have a personality at all. He is possibly the dullest cult figure in the history of English sports. There is nothing controversial about the man.

There are only two things I like about him: his running style (he looks like a child imitating a robot), and the fact he ended the misery of having to watch Ashley Giles. Everything else is meh. I've wanted to like him for a couple of seasons, but I can't do it. A man can't make love to a stone, Monty.

I need something from you. An x factor. A y chromosome. Tell us you slept with a man. Show us your third nipple. Start sledging in pig Latin. Take big bags of wickets. Regale us with tales as your life as a CIA operative. Give us something, Monty.

If not, then I'm afraid you're done here. I have already started seeing a younger man. Adil is the twice the spinner you are, which means he is a leggie. He can actually bat, and he comes from Yorkshire. Plus he is way more exotic than you are.

Monty, you are going on the "players we hate" list, mostly because we don't have a "players we meh" list. Monty, if that is your real name, if you want to come off the list, start performing like a cult figure, or at least give us a rest from the Ashley Giles impersonation.

May 21 - Hey Jardine, leave our Vics alone

Adam Hollioake, Alan Mullally, and Craig White are obviously all champions of English cricket. Hollioake was the best English captain since Grace. Mullally was the best left arm bowler ever. And Craig White was probably the best all rounder England has had since Tony Greig.

Because of the trail-blazing path these three heroes made, England has yet again looked to Victoria to find a champion. This time it is Darren "Eyelids" Pattinson. The man, who was on a rooftop in Dandenong 12 months ago, is now leading the county league tally with an impressive 15 wickets after just eight matches. The rub is that Eyelids has an English passport, which means he can play for the old dart if they ask him nicely. For England's quota system, three non-English accented players per team, Pattinson is perfect.

It's been a while since Mullally took the new ball for England; so let me give the English some new tips on how to handle their new Victorian recruit. You will need more than one Victorian bowler, because the first one will get injured thinking about bowling. The second one will get injured thinking about replacing the first one, so best you have three.

Then you will need Rodney Hogg to psych him up in his mentalist's chamber known as the lunacy room. No Victorian can bowl fast without some time alone with Rodney. After that you need a keeper who can dive in front of first slip. For Victorian bowlers this is like Viagra. And finally you will need to be a good team on paper that never wins anything. Oh good; you've got that covered already.

Usually I would be angry at England for poaching our Eyelids, but as long as they leave Dirty Dirk Nannes alone, it's ok by me. After all, fast bowlers grow on trees here; we don't even have to go into modelling agencies to find them, like they do in the UK.

May 23 - When a hundred means you've failed

The English media were whipping themselves up into a frenzy over Mark Ramprakash's potential 100th First Class 100. I was not.

Disclaimer: If you're a Surrey fan, you may want to switch off now.

Mark Ramprakash played 52 Tests. The same as Don Bradman. Bradman just pipped him in the number of centuries made. By 27. Ramprakash made two in 52 Tests at an average of 27. For younger readers, this may be confusing, as surely a team as well-oiled and professional as England wouldn't allow a man to dance his way to such a bad record. But they did.

The thing is, everyone knows Ramps can bat, especially Ramps. One hundred came against Warne, Lee, Dizzy and McGrath (flat pitch not withstanding). The other against Ambrose, Walsh, Bishop and the great Nixon McClean. Now he has been stuck on 99 first class hundreds for the last few weeks, English county fans are on the edge of their cups of tea in anticipation.

I have always thought making 100 first class hundreds is a failure. There have been players like Grace and Gooch who did it while being very good Test players. The last man to do it was Graeme Hick, the man that Merv Hughes ruined, who batted at Test level like an undecided lemming. Had Ramps and Hick had 12 year Test careers, like they both had the talent to, they would never had reached the 100 first class hundreds mountain top.

Who among us would rather be a statistical anomaly, instead of a fixture of their country's middle order? When Ramps reaches this milestone, there will be a lot of head nodding, back-slapping and praise for this dancing man. But for some of us, we will see this as his ultimate failure. Of course, his wife may think he's had bigger failures.

May 24 - Built like Adonis, tastes like sugar and food colouring

Freddie Flintoff, built like a rugby player, bowls like a superstar, bats like a rugby player.
Matthew Hayden, built like a Frank Miller character, bats like a Frank Miller villain.
Shane Watson, built like a Calvin Klein model, plays like a Calvin Klein model.
Jacob Oram, built like the Perfect Boyfriend, bats like an axeman, bowls like a ballerina.

What do all these players have in common, other than they are the male equivalent of Amazonian women? That's right my intelligent regular reader, they are all jellybean players.

A jellybean player is built like Tarzan, and plays like Shane (Watson). The physio knows their moles by touch. Ice baths are how they relax. And they sometimes have relapses from injury. They are too athletic, too muscular, and too fit to play international cricket.

Cricket is the place for the overweight. The dreadfully skinny. The normal-sized, with large behinds. These are the ideal sizes for cricketers. Someone fit, strong, and healthy is just testing fate by playing cricket.

All these players have had a terrible recent run with injuries, because they are not made for this world. Freddie Flintoff should be a pack scrum forward 5/8th (someone with a thick neck told me of that) type guy. Hayden should be clubbing seals in Alaska. Shane should be stripping naked for photo shoots more often. And Oram should take his rightful place as the thinking woman's Fabio.

Cricket is tough on fit men.

May 25 - Are Australia Australia?

Australia were doing well on the scoreboard in the West Indies, but the cracks were everywhere.

What have we known about Australia for the last ten years?

Arrogant. Organised. Clever. Brutal. Hungry. Champions.

What do we know about the new Australia?

Careful. Professional. Fragile. Nervous. Defensive. Talented.

Australia had a run rate of 1.7 when they lost four wickets to the Windies. Think about how many times you've seen Australia bat that slowly. Australia has used a nightwatchman twice in this game. How many times did Australia use a nightwatchman under Steve Waugh?

Australia has one champion batsman in their team. The '80s were the last time that happened. Australia has a makeshift opener. Justin Langer was a makeshift opener that worked out ok, but Katich doesn't look like doing the same.

Australia has no champion bowlers. Wait let me check. No, none. Brett Lee's average is 29, no ten wicket hauls (yet). Clark has come into a good team and performed well; no ten wicket hauls. MacGill is better than average, and a great wicket taker, but lets the pressure off too easily; two ten wicket hauls. Johnson is still not good with a red ball; never taken more than six wickets in a match.

They are still the best side in the world. But only because no one else is good enough. India, Sri Lanka and South Africa, all have glaring holes in their line-ups, which at this stage is all that is keeping Australia on top.

Australia smashed Sri Lanka. Australia were two-nil up against India. And South Africa has their chance after Australia visit India.

This current line up is probably not the worst side they have had in the last ten years, but it's close, and it has less match winners than any side since '92. Ponting wanted to stamp his mark on this side; finally he is, because he has a whole new side. They are cautious, professional, well-researched, fiery, but they are not as good as they were. The list of players they are missing from three years ago is huge.

G McGrath, statistically the best fast bowler in Australian history.
S Warne, arguably the best spinner ever.
A Gilchrist, best batting keeper ever.
J Gillespie, steady as a train fast bowling bagman.
D Martyn, one time unbeatable number four.
J Langer, the punchy opening batsman.
M Hayden, the bullying Christian warrior, who is temporarily out of action.

Ponting is going to be tested this series. Australia might still win three-zip, but he will have to keep improving as a captain. Questions continue to be asked, and Australia keep passing, but the marks are getting lower and lower.

May 28 - Daniel Flynn, no nansy pansy

Daniel Flynn, a young gritty New Zealander, copped a smack in the head from from James Anderson; it was a brutal hit.

According to William Shatner you don't want to be one. Jacob Oram has spent the best part of his career with the tag of "NP" never far away from him. Jason Gillespie would play if he had a broken leg in the second part of the career to dispel the myth that he was.

Daniel Flynn better get used to it. Cricket, Test cricket, is not a place for the soft. Facing Brett Lee, Dale Steyn or Malinga is a test of courage. Flynn got hit, he lost a tooth or two, he suffered concussion, he threw up for hours, he could not sleep, and he didn't bat. On the face of it he looks soft.

The truth is that he wanted to bat in the second innings and he wasn't allowed. It may place too much importance on him to say it cost the victory, but it sure as hell didn't help. Educated cricket fans will know Flynn wanted to bat, but everyone else will label him soft. And once pronounced soft, the label sticks for a long time.

Flynn looks anything but soft. He looks like he should be beating up bigger kids at an arcade parlour. While this will sound harsh, he reminds me of Justin Langer. A scrapper, a fighter, a tough little bastard. So why hold him back?

Australia spent Langer's whole career putting him in harms way. He debuted as a 21-year-old against the Windies, and loved it. He fielded at short leg for almost ten years. He was told if he got hit in the head one more time he could die; he continued to play. One time Langer almost got killed in South Africa by an Ntini bouncer, the doctors told Ponting that Langer could not bat. With eight wickets down and ten runs to get Langer padded up, and Ponting told him he would try and restrain him from getting to the field, or declare on him.

Australia won without losing another wicket. Langer said afterwards had Ponting stopped him from batting he would have never talked to him again.

That is the sort of player you want on your side. New Zealand needs more players who will die to win a Test match. They have the bling (Taylor, Oram and Prince Brendon McCullum), now they need the grunt. Flynn seems to be potentially grunt-like, so let him play with a sore head, and see how he goes. He still has plenty of teeth left.

May 29 - Workmanlike, pot, kettle, Vaughan

This was the post that eventually won me July's Best of the Blogs in the Wisden Cricketer.

Before the first test Michael Vaughan called the New Zealand XI workmanlike. Some Kiwis got offended. Most people think he is right, but I would say most people are idiots. After two Tests it has been proved that if any team is workmanlike it's England.

New Zealand has Taylor, an attacking batsman who can win a game at any time. Oram, one of the most destructive big hitters in the game. And Prince Brendon McCullum, the most exciting batsman on earth.

Who does England have that can compare to this blingy trio?

I would say pound for pound England has the most workmanlike side on earth. KP was a former most exciting batsman on earth, but once he was at the English firm for long enough they made him an in house lawyer, after he couldn't cut it in private practice in South Africa.

The English firm

Strauss, an experienced HR manager who calls himself wing commander and everyone laughs at him.
Cook is the fresh young graduate in IT who everyone suspects wears mascara.
Vaughan is the CEO, who thinks he is still the young buck but all his shirts have yellow stains around the neck.
Bell is the salesman everyone talks up as exciting because he went to a rave once, and who wears way too much cologne.
Collingwood is the accountant; no one works longer hours for less productivity.
Ambrose is the new marketing manager: started with a bang, but so did the last four guys in his job.
Broad, the son of a former employee, works in dispatch. Everyone talks about how young he is; no one talks about how good he is.
Sidebottom is the factory foreman; without him the company would cease to exist.
Panesar is the office manager who wears odd socks and novelty ties, but sits on the net all day looking for a girlfriend.
Anderson is the guy who drives the forklift into the walls, but the girls in the office still think he is dreamy.

There are no players in there who are genuine superstars (at the moment), no players who are worth the admission price on their own, and no players who can inspire great deeds.

New Zealand definitely has some blue-collar players (O'Brien and How are as workmanlike as you can get), but McCullum is far more exciting than anyone wearing the pristine whites for England at the moment.

England are like an episode of The Office with the cast of Neighbours playing all the parts. Actually, that would be more entertaining to watch.

May 29 - The slide

Australia continue to win against the Windies in an unconvincing manner.

Recently much has been made of Australia's slide. Most of this is because of Stuart MacGill's newfound ability not to land his leg break, Mitchell Johnson and his line three foot wide outside off stump, their sick reliance on Matthew Hayden, and let us not forget Michael Clarke's dodgy form in pressure situations.

I have been talking about this for months now. But how bad is it?

In how many countries would a player like Shaun Marsh not be good enough to be picked in their top eight batsmen? And realistically, David Hussey would still be ahead of him on the list, so Marsh may not even be in Australia's top nine batsmen. We the people all know this is rubbish, and that he should be currently preparing to open for Australia ahead of the Krab Katich, or at least carrying the drinks and trying some rum instead of Brad Hodge.

It does show the amazing depth that Australia still has, even without the champions at the top. Shane Watson is probably the best performing player in the IPL, if Marsh isn't, and he is not in Australia's One Day squad. Both David Hussey and Luke Pomersbach have been less dominant than Marsh and Watson, but they have both played innings that have showed they belong.

You may ask where the young Australian bowlers are. Well, Brett Geeves got spanked every time he got a gig. And almost every other young Australian bowler is a physical basket case, but Peter Sizzle (Siddle), and Dougie Bollinger take wickets on one leg.

Marsh still stands out. Not just because of the runs he has made, or the strike rate he has maintained, but because he hasn't slogged. He has kept his technique, and he has batted like a serious batsman-type batsman, which means he may turn out to be a real player on the international circuit.

Want more than IPL proof? Well the English sports writers are already worried about him for the Ashes. Ok the English are always worried about the Ashes, but in Marsh, they have just cause. And by 2013 Shaun's little brother Mitchell will be in England, probably batting at number three.

Cricket With Balls, monitoring the demise of Australia one MacGill long hop at a time.

June 2 - Lord Stuey, a tribute, a bagging, a goodbye

Lord Stuey was like an unromantic and grumpy version of Mr Darcy from Pride and Prejudice. Unfortunately for him he walked into a dressing room that was more Mad Max than Jane Austen. He was never ever going to fit in, and some will say he didn't have to.

They could be right: 200 wickets @ 28 with a titillating strike rate should have been enough. But the Australian public has an image of its cricketers, and Stuey MacGill was not it. The fact a born and bred Australian could be thought of as less Australian than a West Indian dreadlocked Pommy born player (Andrew Symonds) says it all.

Stuey is Australian, but he just ain't the Australian that most people automatically think of. He was too educated. Quiet when he should be loud, and loud when he should be quiet. He sledged his team-mates more than he sledged the opposition. He was sulky. Too sure of himself. Wanted to distance himself from the sport that made him. Took political stands. Hated Murdoch papers. Got excited in odd moments. Bowled too many bad balls. Had an air that alienated sports fans. Sometimes he looked angrier getting a wicket than he did getting hit for four. His long sleeves and correctly enunciated words were of another era, and another country. The average Australian cricket fan thought he was a wanker.

He wasn't the sort of bloke you'd have a beer with, want your sister dating, or could visit Phillip Island with. Stuey was more the kind you'd expect behind the lectern giving a speech on Political Science. Australian cricket is not the place for a man like him, and it showed throughout his whole career. He had the anger, the hunger and the skill to play for Australia, but he just did it differently. At his best he was in the top three leg spinners in the world. At his worst he was uglier than a Chernobyl reunion.

He imparted amazing spin on the ball. When he took wickets, he took bagfuls. But he was erratic, he was difficult and he could lose the plot like few before him. His failures were extravagantly wonderful, including bowling the West Indies to a record fourth innings run chase. Team-mates, the media and fans couldn't work him out. The fact that Brad Hogg, a man with 1/80th the skill level, was more well-liked, tells the story.

He was Lord Stuey, the man with the golden hands. Part old world spinner, part new world intellectual. A man who preferred a sip of merlot to a skull of XXXX. A man who refused to fit in. A man who very rarely bored you. You may have loved him. You may have hated him. But how many people had no opinion on him at all?

Stuey, it has been a pleasure to bag you, worship you, laugh at you, laugh with you and watch you. You have earned your place in the Leg Spinning Valhalla.

June 2 - Bryce McGain's first comments on Lord Stuey's departure

"No comment."

You heard it here first. This is a real quote; it is not made up. True story.

June 3 - Asif picks up the wrong bag

Mohammad Asif leaves the IPL, and takes too much luggage with him back to Pakistan.

Mohammad Asif has been taken into custody after being suspected of carrying opium. The PCB are being tight-lipped about the controversy so far. I think this is a simple case of Mohammad picking up the wrong bag. He meant to pick up the bag with the performance-enhancing drugs, but instead picked up Shoaib's overnight bag. Apparently he was not going to use the opium to get high, but just wanted to test India's opium against that good shit he gets from Afghanistan.

Asif, Heath Ledger's favourite cricketer, had to fly from Mumbai to Pakistan via Dubai, which of course is why he wanted the opium. Two flights without opium is never a good idea. Personally I blame the Mumbai Indians for all of this. Not because he played for them, but because their team was boring as hell.

June 5 - In bed with King Probot

Disclaimer: Yes, this is one of my perverted posts, not for the kiddies, or the Mormons.

A while ago I wrote a post about everyone's favourite player, Jacques Kallis, in the bedroom. It's unfair to pick on just Jacques' boudoir activities, because many cricketers have sex.

So I shall turn this into a series.

Mike Hussey, or King Probot as he is known around these parts, is a patient man. He would wait for ten years to sleep with his dream girl. And when he got there he would be super prepared. Were you his dream girl, he would know exactly what you wanted.

You would be whisked off to some romantic hotel with a view over whatever you like to look at, be it beach, mountain, or city park. Upon entering the room, he would have set up your favourite chocolates, drinks and music and would have the candles set up just they way the were in your fantasies. He would be attentive to your every need.

You would receive all the special attention that you ladies have been looking for. Back massages. A bath where he washes your hair, romantically, not roughly like that episode where Steve hurts Miranda. If your mother calls, he will wait patiently for you to finish talking to her, perhaps even rubbing your feet during that time.

Then, after pressing play on Robbie Williams' "Swing When You're Winning", he will start with the kissing. Long passionate kisses, until he feels you actually swoon. Then he leads you to the canopy bed, which he carefully spread rose petals over earlier. Then he would go into the foreplay; this he is willing to spend hours on, but he will read your mood, and tailor the foreplay to suit what you require.

From there he will move into the love-making, where he is technically proficient in every aspect that you desire. He knows the exact way to pleasure you; he never forces too hard or too soft. He takes risks, but they are calculated risks that he knows you will more than likely enjoy. The session is long, superhumanly long, but he never raises a sweat, and looks determined to finish the job, which he does several times over even when he struggles through a difficult middle patch.

Afterwards you lie back on this canopy bed, in this perfect hotel room, with the rose petals sticking to your thigh, Robbie crooning away, looking out the window on your perfect view. You think about this session, and how it was almost perfect in every way, nothing was left to chance and in terms of quality and quantity it was everything you had ever hoped for.

But it is not Mike that you think of. Instead all you can think of is the three minutes you spent in the back of cab with Afridi just before dawn one time. You'd never tell Mike though, he is such a nice guy. He'll call you tomorrow to make sure you're ok, and your mum will love him.

June 11 – The Young & Restless' Beau gets a gig

Beau Casson's debut, and possible last Test match. The first line was purposefully put there to annoy some grammar nazis.

In a very unique decision that has decimated my soul, Beau Casson has been selected for Australia. Due to the lack of Bryce McGain in the touring party, Beau was always going to be picked. Beau's selection is different to most other mistakes Australia makes, in that this was a failure to plan for Lord Stuey's demise. All well and good taking a project player to the Windies, but there was always a chance Stuey would not stay healthy, mentally or physically, for this trip.

But I have more important things to be angry for, the reason is because of Mitchell Johnson's continuing free ride in Test cricket. Johnson's form is figuratively rubbish. Yet he keeps getting a gig.

Beau Casson has to come into a side as a debutante who is lucky to get a game and he only has two other bowlers who are up to Test match standard to help him. Oh and Haddin is playing, bugger.

June 11 - The narcotics anonymous XI

1. Mohammed Asif was not happy with the effect steroids had on his demeanour, so sent down an opium chaser to balance it out, and surprisingly the Dubai Airport officials frowned on this.
2. Herschelle Gibbs tried a bit of Mary Jane in the West Indies. He also likes to drink'n'drive and match fix. He is all class.
3. Ed Giddons was suspended for 18 months after testing positive to cocaine. Best sledge he received was "Don't let them get up your nose, Giddo". Imagine the worst.
4. Stephen Fleming used marijuana as a way to prepare himself for captaincy of the hardest working team in world cricket. No wonder he looked so calm.
5. Lalit Modi, the IPL guru was guilty of cocaine possession in North Carolina and given a two-year sentence (which he didn't serve). The two-year decision had more to do with the kidnapping and assault charges he also pleaded guilty to.
6. Ian Botham admitted to enjoying weed, but denied claims he once got high on cocaine with a Miss Barbados and broke the bed during love-making. Why?
7. West Australian Duncan Spencer was banned for taking the performance enhancing drug nandrolone. His first class bowling average was 39. Enhancing?
8. Maninder Singh the Indian left arm spinner got caught with 1.5 grams of white powder. This apparently had nothing to do with the dodgy LBW he received to tie the tied Test.
9. Shane Warne thought he looked fat and took a diet pill that doubles as a masking agent. Perhaps he should have just eaten less pizza.
10. Adeel Raja, a Holland International, was banned for using finasteride. It's not surprising that a Dutch cricketer had been banned for taking drugs, but all he did was forget to extend the dispensation that had been granted to him previously.
11. Shoaib Ahktar was found with nandrolone in his system, but the PCB didn't seem to mind that much, and once Bob Woolmer died, everyone had more important things to worry about.
12th man Phil Tufnell.
Coach: Brigitte Warne.

June 12 - Michael Hussey, the IPL's biach

Part of the offshoot of the IPL was a Champion's League tournament with sides from most of the Twenty20 competitions in the world. As some players would qualify with more than one side, it became an issue as players were told they could play with their home sides originally.

This site engages in a form of journalism called "We told ya so". Recently I said that Michael Hussey would play for Chennai in the Champion's League thingy, because he likes to please people. He can't play for them though, as Australia are preparing for their tour of India, and daddy Sutherland (Cricket Australia's James Sutherland) said "no".

But, this is what Hussey said: "I'm a Western Australia boy through and through, born and bred, so if I'm playing a competition I'd probably prefer to play for Western Australia. But if the rules state that I'm playing for Chennai, then I'm very happy to play for them as well".

At this stage there are no rules, and more importantly, he has not signed a contract saying he is willing to put the IPL first. He went on to say that he was originally told he could play for Western Australia if they made it. "To hear something different seems a bit strange to me," Hussey said, "but obviously if that's the rules, that's the rules".

Stop talking about the rules, King Probot. There are no rules. If he told you that you'd be able to play for your state, and that there is no contract stating otherwise, then Modi can place his hand up his own behind, rip out his prostate, and lick it.

Hussey would never want to cause a fuss, and is probably secretly thrilled that the decision has been made for him. Stuart Law on the other hand has taken a slightly different stance on the ban on ICL players from the Champions League: "I'm going to play and there's nothing anyone can do to stop me".

Good luck with that mate.

I do agree with his stance, and he does make valid points: "there are no rules for the Champions League yet so how can anybody disqualify us? All I'm trying to do is earn my living in this big, bad world".

But I restate my previous comment. Good luck with that mate.

Modi may back down on his home team stance, but you'd think Godzilla herself would be needed for him to let the enemy into his private league.

June 12 - L Ron Stanford

Allen Stanford's first real mention on the blog.

Not since Battlefield Earth has there been bigger waste of money than this 20 million dollar game. Stanford has raided his piggy bank so that one of The England and the Stanford All Star XI will be rewarded. For the sake of Twenty20 continuity, the Stanford All Star XI is being renamed the Stanford XI All Star, (think Kings XI Punjab).

I don't have a problem with 20 million dollars being spent on one game of cricket. It's about time cricketers cashed in like other major sports stars do. They certainly make enough for sponsors and TV networks. But, 20 million dollars and all we can get is an England v West Indies (SXIAS) Twenty20 game?

Neither side made the semis of the Twenty20 World (Cup) Championships. One side has never won a One Day World Cup, the other side won a couple when John Lennon was around. They are ranked at six and eight in the current One Day rankings. Most importantly they fail the one big test when talking about 20 million dollar games: neither side has it in them to provide 20 million dollars worth of entertainment.

This could be the worst value-for-money deal since the last John Travolta film. Bravo, KP, Freddie Flintoff, Edwards and Gayle aside, these two teams have the personality of a plastic tree. That is being unkind to plastic trees.

For 20 million dollars you want sex, excitement, and controversy.

Not Sidebottom bowling to the Chrab. Or Jimmy Anderson looking smarmily at Sarwan. What we have here is a 20 million dollar budget, and an eight dollar product.

June 13 - I shook up the world

'Bout freakin time. Cricket With Balls has been placed in The Wisden Cricketer, and she will never be the same again. She will tell her friends that was just a one off thing, but the truth is, she likes it dirty, and she will be back for more.

Of course I couldn't have done it alone; The Wisden Cricketer even mentions the peer pressure you, the readers, put on her. So thank you to everyone who commented, on this post especially, but all comments really and thanks to everyone who reads the blog regularly.

Extra special thanks to that dude who sent me a nude photo of Natalie Portman.

June 16 - I can't quit you

Pakistan suspended Shoaib Ahktar, for, well, for being Shoaib Ahktar, but in his absence the heart grew fonder.

Ahktar's return is only 18 months away. Mark it down on your calendar. The question is, can we wait 18 months?

Andre Nel may be finished forever. Harbhajan Singh and Sreesanth are surely not going to get caught being freakin' morons again. Jesse Ryder may never recover. Mark Cosgrove can't make a run for South Australia. Freddie Flintoff can't find a spot in England's side. And Lasith Malinga doesn't get caught with drugs or hit team-mates with bats.

Don't tell anyone I said so, but I miss Shoaib. I still despise him for being a lazy soft fucker. But I miss his antics. I miss his stupid statements. His stubborn refusal of baldness. His photo opportunities with Geoff Lawson. His telling the Pakistan people not to revolt for his cause. His excuses. His arrogance. His part-time performances.

And most of all I miss his personality off the field. Because he had one. Sure he was a selfish drug-taking playboy, but he was our selfish drug taking playboy, and who are we left with?

Kyle Mills? Brett Lee? Dale Steyn? Chaminda Vaas?

None of the bowlers are ready to be Shoaib. They are professional cricketers. We want playboys, angry mentalists, drunkards, and fatties. Shoaib was every bad cricket habit rolled into one. So I beg of the Pakistan Cricket Board: let the boy play. We need someone to bag, hate, love and laugh at again, and Younis Khan and Muhammad Asif combined cannot do the job.

June 17 - Australia win two-zip

Australia beat the West Indies.

That's the title, but the story had a bit more to it than that. Ricky finally admitted his bowlers had come back to the pack. What he didn't say was that Johnson is currently not a Test match bowler and they have no idea what they are going to do about a spinner.

On flat decks, which are the standard these days, Australia does not have the artillery to get out good batsman. Brett Lee is the best fast bowler on earth, but no one bowls longer, more hostile spells for fewer wickets. Stuart Clark is McGrath lite. Fewer pouts, fewer wickets. Mitchell Johnson took five wickets in the first two Tests, but the wickets aren't his major problem, the problem is that every time he bowls, all the pressure that Clark and Lee have built up just fades away.

Casson is ?

The batting still works; different soldiers, but they still make runs. It just isn't as pretty as it used to be.

Over in the other camp they missed Gayle. Chanderpaul is still the man. And the others, Sarwan and Bravo included, do melt under extreme heat. A top five of Gayle, Chatterjoon, Sarwan, Marshall and Chanderpaul could work. Edwards, Taylor, Bravo and Powell is a fair bowling line up on its day. They hit Australia at the perfect time, their first trip without the stars, and they gave them a shake.

Their recent form is impressive. Winning a Test in South Africa. Drawing one-all with the Sri Lankans who had just pantsed England. And now pushing Australia in all three games.

They play New Zealand next, and they should feel they are at least the equals of New Zealand if not slightly ahead on recent form. The West Indies will feel quite rightly that they are improving, but they still have a fair way to travel before becoming a Test team again.

Australia shouldn't worry as much as people will want them too, but more than they are.

June 21 - My lunch with Joe Average

My first steps towards being a proper cricket journalist begin with interviewing one of the biggest names in world cricket, Bryce McGain.

Cricket With Balls is not a journalistic institution. However, due to recent developments and so forth, I was in a position to interview one of Cricket With Balls' favourite sons, Bryce McGain. It is fitting that Bryce is my first interview, as he was the first, and only, player to receive the "Cricket With Balls' Own" tag.

Bryce opted to meet in a seaside café. The view of the ocean was horrid, but luckily the junkies made up for it. For those who are interested, he wore a blue hoodie, and had just come from a session. Bryce is a nice guy, which is lucky, given his other nickname of Nice Bryce. Early on we covered the important things, like whether Dirty Dirk knows where he is bowling it (answer is no), and about how it came to pass that Bryce played for Denmark.

The Denmark story was a bit unexciting, but perhaps because I was expecting him to say, "my father was an Earl of Copenhagen, and one day I got a call from Princess Mary asking me to do my duty for the national side or I would end up beheaded". He was playing club cricket over there, and was picked to be the overseas player in the tournament that Scotland, the Netherlands, Denmark and Ireland play against the county sides, of which the name has eluded me. They must have had a strong side as Bryce batted in the middle order. The fact he made 50 also tells you of the level of the opposition; no Brett Lees around.

Bryce is now a full time cricketer, leaving his job as ANZ IT bagman behind him. Hence why he can sit in a café and talk shit about cricket for a couple of hours. The one thing I noticed, and it happened repeatedly, was Bryce's constant reference to himself as Joe Average.

At first I thought it might have been a reference to his alter ego, some sort of superhero who puts out fires and saves kittens by night. But no, this is how Bryce saw his life before Terry Jenner, Warne and I started name-dropping him. Notice how I slipped in my name into the same line as Shane Warne so smoothly.

Back then he was Bryce McGain, father, bank employee and cricket enthusiast. Now he is Bryce McGain, the Facebook kid, Cricket With Balls' Own, Nice Bryce, and potential

Test cricketer for Australia. Surprisingly enough, no one came up for an autograph during our time together.

Although the Asian lady sitting next to us did say leggie at one stage. Or she was ordering a veggie burger.

June 23 - The prophets explained

Jesus was a wicket keeper. Soft hands that got worse with age. A scratchy start, but he was 30 before you knew it. Willing to sacrifice his innings for the good of the team.

L Ron Hubbard was a mystery spinner. A lot of talk about the legality of his action. Once worked out, was relatively straightforward. Exiled from the game.

Rael is a leg spinner. His good balls are unplayable. His bad balls are truly horrible. Every team should have one, but only one; no clones allowed.

Joseph Smith was a medium pacer. Not flashy, but he got the wickets. Bowled long spells with several different bowlers rotated at the other end. Liked to bowl uphill.

Moses was an all-rounder. Sometimes he led the attack. Sometimes he took the attack to the opposition. Was quite fickle about the rules of the game.

Muhammad is a cricket administracrat. Invented a new form of the game. He wrote the rule book and did the publicity. People in certain geographical places loved this game so much that they abandoned other forms of it.

June 24 - Changing ends

I am doing what so many Australians do: I am off to cash in on the easy money on offer in the UK. In a few weeks I leave the birthplace of champions, the northern suburbs of Melbourne, for the birthplace of something, London. I have been to London before, but I seemed to spend most of my time drinking with ex-pat Australians who thought they were so freakin' cool to be living in London in a share house with 12 others. Fuckin' tossers. The rest of my time was spent in a Russian mob café eating something they called fish; I took their word for it.

While I am really looking forward to moving to England, I will still miss some things about home. Watching the first Test and trying to work out what Ian Chappell's bugbear for the summer is going to be. Having all my mates ask me to the Boxing Day Test, even though none of them are cricket fans, and they should know I don't go to Test matches to drink.

Sitting alone, or near a certain player's mother at a state game, silently judging the players and the autograph hunters. Going to the MCG 30 times a year. Watching a One

Day game from the Members'. Sitting in a bar arguing with my mate on whether Test cricket is dead. Sitting in the stands with Sime and Big Daddy as Big Daddy does his best to piss off every person sitting around us, while Sime gets fired up over bad techniques and refuses to get the sunscreen. Talking to my dad about how bad Ponting is as a captain.

Collingwood, and AFL football in general. The Epping train line. Ignoring the latest Australian film. Trams.

I should arrive in England just in time for the South African tour. And then Andre and I shall take over the world.

Houhahahaaaahaa...

June 28 - KP's first team meeting

Kevin Pietersen stood in as captain of the One Day side when Paul Collingwood was amazingly suspended, not castrated, for slow over rates.

KP: Hello everyone, what's my name?
Everyone: KP.
KP: Good, ok team tactics, play like me, at all times. I want you to look good, be confident, groom yourself well, and have an uptight swagger.
Everyone: Ok.
KP: What's my name?
Everyone: KP.
KP: Nice, Ryan, you'll need a haircut if you want to bowl. Jimmy, ever thought of an accent? Cooky, go easy on the eye makeup, don't wanna upstage me now. Belly, keep playing as usual, no threat there. Ravi and Owais, due to my quota system you have missed out and two South African Englishmen will be brought in. Luke, I want you to bat stoically, really knuckle in, no big shots. Swanny, you're playing as a batsman, I'll take your overs. Broady, you'll bat at three. And Timmy, you're doing super.

In the field I want you to be alert, but not alarmed; if the ball is not in play, I want your eyes on me. When I do something good, I want a minimum of three players to come over and pat my back. Also, if grass or dirt get on my clothes, I want someone to subtly brush it off in the form of a back slap. Instead of saying "come on chaps", or "let's go England", I wanna hear "come on KP's men". The game will go like this: I will win the toss, and we will bat, you will let me come in at the 11 over mark. I will do my thing, and we will make between 380 and 400. I will do a quick press conference about being the first batsman to make a One Day double ton. During the break, Wrighty and Broady, you will peel grapes and wash me. Thoroughly. In the field I will bowl the over after each wicket. So if Ryan takes a wicket first over, I will bowl the second, excellent. After our victory I will give a few more press conferences and talk about how much it means for me to play with, um, England. Good, ok, now I have organised a team bonding session at a day spa, they will be doing hair, nails, and skin care. Remember

boys, this is your nation you're playing for, but today I want you to play for something way more important; me. What's my name?
Everyone: KP.
KP: Damn skippy.

June 28 - In bed with Monty

You're walking through the supermarket. Picking up your loaf of white bread, a dark figure bumps into you. He knocks your basket to the ground and quickly picks it up for you. You can't help but look in his basket. He has all sorts of foods in there, foods you can't believe, foods you have never dared to try.

He's different. He's not like anyone you've dated before. He is exotic, mysterious, and in your mind capable of taking you to places you've never been to. But you have a boyfriend, and although he is no Mr Excitement and has no mystery or exoticness at all, he has given you support and helped you in times of need.

You flirt with Monty and even take his number, but you leave him at the supermarket and go home and have safe and boring sex with your boyfriend, if he's not too tired. Monty is never far from your thoughts. One day, when your boyfriend tells the same boring story, it just clicks; he is never going to change.

You need excitement, you need mystery, and you need Monty. Monty comes over, and he is punctual, polite and pleasant. Not the most brilliant conversationalist, but that's not why he's there. You egg him on, you talk him up, and you stroke his ego so much he performs exactly as you believe he would.

He performs to his maximum, but a lot of that is all the ego-stroking you provide. The sex is better than you have had in a long time, and right in that moment it is bliss. He puts it in the right areas and in your mind it is the best sex you've had, even better than those few times with the drunken poet ten years ago.

In bed Monty is a considerate lover, although not always brilliant with his hands. He looks after your needs, he is patient, and on his day he can be quite exceptional. The problem is that he's extremely noisy all the time, so much so that you find it hard to tell when he's reached his goal and when he's just making noise. And when he does get there, he celebrates like no man you've ever known.

You realise that he essentially does the same thing every time, and sometimes that comes off, and other times it fails badly. Slowly the novelty of his exotic nature starts to wear off, and you realise he is just another boring boyfriend. Sure he was caring, and your mum liked him, but he didn't light your fire. You are in a rut, you have no reason to leave him, but he just isn't the man you thought he was.

You think rationally about the situation. "He does the job I require, and he is a nice guy, I really should be happy to have found him".

Then one day you meet a really exotic young chap from Yorkshire and…

June 30 - Joe Average, the thinker

More snippets from the interview with Bryce McGain.

Bryce McGain is a thinker. I don't say that just because he wears glasses. He has theories on things, and they don't come straight from the cliché mill. The really interesting stuff though was his theory on bowling. He was talking about how, if he plays in India, they will try to destroy him.

In his mind, once the ball leaves your hand, that's it. You can't control what happens next. You plan and then try and execute a ball to get the batsman out, but once the ball leaves your hand the batsman is in control.

As a spinner, you can land the perfect ball and the batsman can put it in the stand. I think too many bowlers, especially young bowlers, worry more about what the batsman will do than actually what they are doing. Your job is to get the ball in the right position and then hope it's good enough to make the batsman make an error.

You really can't do any better than bowling a good ball; whether it gets hit for six or gets a wicket is beyond your control once it leaves your hand. It's a different way of looking at bowling. Other bowlers may think the same way, but I've never heard anyone explain it like this. At the end he said "no matter how far they hit me for six it won't change the fact that I know I can bowl".

He doesn't just wear the glasses just for the ladies; I think he reads books and stuff.

July 1 - South Africa's scared little boys

Mr Panic (a regular commenter here, not a jazz musician from the '60s), alerted me a few days ago to an article in The Times about Neil McKenzie. I can't find it now, but it talked about McKenzie's OCD before and during his innings.

They include, but are not limited to, taping his bat to the change room ceiling, making sure the toilet seats are down when he goes out to bat and not stepping on the white lines out on the ground. If I was a coach and I had a player with those problems, I wouldn't counsel him, mollycoddle him or get him assistance. I'd take him out the back and shoot him. Not killing him, just a flesh wound to the thigh.

The point is, South Africa do not have mentally tough batsman. They appear tough. But scratch the surface and they are all nervous wrecks.

Cullinan kept talking the talk even though Warne had shown him to be a cupcake.

Gibbs, who can be easily convinced to cheat, and then forget about it eight minutes later.
Smith, who acts like Matt Hayden on the field, and off it as the poor nerdy kid who can't find a woman.
Kallis: like I have to explain.
Cronje: the devil made me do it, what, the devil made you be a whiny little Jesus freak?
Amla: just kill Smith and take over the side already.
Prince: the dude wears mittens.
Dippenaar, Rudolph, and Bacher are hardly worth mentioning.

So why do they win matches?

They quite regularly have the men who can take 20 wickets.

Ntini: as if you'd wanna be in a back alley with him.
Nel: as if you'd wanna be in a mental ward with him.
Steyn: as if you'd wanna be in a men's day spa with him.

These are real men. Fast bowling men's men. Not mitten-wearing Jesus freaks who tape bats to the ceiling. Well I hope not, as it would ruin the point of this article.

Bowlers win matches. Batsman sign bat sponsors. Wicketkeepers get the girls. True story.

July 2 - Ask agony uncle

Mark Ramprakash had still not made his 100th First Class 100.

This is the first in the Agony Uncle series. Where we try to help a cricketer in need.

"Hi CWB,
Hope you can help me, seems I have developed some performance anxiety issues when trying to consummate my relationship for the 100th time. What is your advice? Please help me.
Dancin' Man, Surrey."

Thanks for contacting us Dancin' Man, we will do our best.

It was easy for you. Very few have ever done it better or more often. You breezed through it for so long. Now you are about to make it to a huge milestone and every one is talking about you and your prowess.

Suddenly, all these paranoid thoughts come to mind. What if I don't do it right? What if Graham Gooch wants me to come to his house? What if I don't last long enough? What if I turn into Graeme Hick? What if there is no climax? Then before you know it, things go completely awry.

And thus begins the vicious circle, a self-fulfilling prophecy if you will, because this one time leads to other discouraging thoughts: Oh my God, what's wrong with me? Is it going to keep happening? I really am a horrible lover and batsman... Stop it, NOW!

What's happening here?

Performance anxiety is a very common problem where men (and yes, even batsmen) acquire brutal anxiety when it comes time to engage in strenuous activity. What ultimately happens is that you become so fully engrossed in the fear of the inability to perform, that it ends up overtaking what should've been a spontaneous flow of cover drives.

The fear of not being able to perform sexually can affect guys in a variety of ways:

- They tend to avoid sexual encounters
- They can develop low self-esteem
- The lack of scoring ability
- The career may deteriorate
- Unable to put away balls on the pads
- It can lead to sexual dysfunction
- It can lead to piss-taking posts written about them

But you know what? That's not the way things have to be. The mind is a very powerful tool and today you're going to learn how to use it not only to maintain an erection, but be the batsman your county always knew you could be.

Take a look inside.

Stress can stem from anywhere: your family is getting on your nerves, reality TV shows, the fact everyone one in the country with a keyboard has written about your special occasion, Mark Butcher, your team is about to be relegated, Patrick Kidd won't stop calling you... you get the general idea.

The fact that these things are weighing heavily on your mind is deterring you from delving into your experience at the crease with no holds barred. And once you're able to leave all the muck on the outside and let the pitch be your sanctuary, you will finally overcome your performance anxiety.

If you are having trouble with your sexual performance please go to AskMen.com.

If you are having trouble making your 100th 100, just make it already.

July 4 - In bed with Daniel Vettori

Miriam looks into the thinking women's spinner.

He comes home to your tastefully furnished apartment (filled with books and art), with a bunch of flowers, and spends a few minutes telling you about his day and politely enquiring about yours.

You'd play a game of Scrabble, he'd finish the Sudoku you struggled with earlier. You'd share a bottle of wine. After dinner he'd wash up. Then you'd both read; you'd pick up "A Suitable Boy" and linger especially on the political bits, whilst he reads "A Brief History of Time" (original unabridged version, borrowed from Stuart MacGill).

You'd listen to music. You'd put on Hayden string quartets, he'd remove the CD and put in Arensky piano trios.

In preparation, you've put on his favourite outfit: a pencil skirt, white shirt, pearls, little cardigan, high heels, hair piled up on your head, glasses even though you don't need them. Then, he'd perform a Haka in front of you. You'd say for the millionth time "Daniel, for the love of God, can't we just have sex already" and he'd say "yes, but why the hell should rugby get all the NZ sporting glory?".

When he'd finished the Haka, he'd take off your hairclip with one hand and your glasses with another, allowing your hair to cascade down over your shoulders, and would say "Why, I never realised you were so beautiful!". You'd then say your line "And I never knew you were so …. manly".

Finally, you get down to it.

He has a habit of sticking out his tongue, but in a cute way, not in a horrid way like that Aussie spinner you once encountered. He mixes delicacy and strength, and is particularly skilled with his fingers, but he's really good with the wood too. Genuine all-round ability. He'd tell you that he loves how you love him for his mind, while you gaze at his body.

However, there is trouble in paradise.

For a quickie, he's fine. In fact, he's one of the best. But for a satisfyingly drawn-out session, with plenty of time spent at the crease, you can forget it, because he's only able to manage it once. He's only EVER able to manage it once.

You'd have one really exciting go with him, it would look like you were on the way to a second, but any attempt at prolonging the action so as to get a result would cause a hopelessly limp collapse.

To get you through the night, you dream about the day that he swore repeatedly in public, and make a note to press the blue "keep" button on your Skyplus for the highlights of the fourth ODI. That gets him worked up like nothing else, even better than the specialist stuff you downloaded from the internet.

The next Friday night, the girls come over for chardonnay, romcoms, chocolate and facepacks, and you get talking about your men. They all say how much they envy you, how your husband is the hottest, how they love the geek chic, how he's so CUTE and CLEVER and FUNNY and SENSITIVE.

You laugh and smile, and raise your glass with them. After they've gone, though, you listen to "I've been to paradise but I've never been to me", unlock your secret bedside table drawer and think of Shane Bond.

July 4 - You are an agent of change, for the better

Take your pants off. No really. Your top too. David Hussey is playing his first real game for Australia. Let it swing. Or them swing. Our petition has finally come to fruition.

This is a chance for global nakedness. Getting a new Victorian in the Australian side is like getting the Palestinians and the Israelis to agree on Jerusalem, only way tougher. And you did it: by reading this blog you initiated change.

You're a revolutionary reader. Like Che Guevara, only not cool, violent or on a t-shirt. David Hussey is batting at number six, behind his brother King Probot, which based on batting styles is odd.

So now I hope for some sort of Victorian type collapse so the Future PM David Hussey can save the day. Stay tuned. Watch this space. Etc.

July 7 - Don't get too excited

Mendis takes India apart, and I unravel the sexcapde you started with David Hussey's promotion.

Turn the video camera off. Uncuff your partner. Refrigerate your whipped cream. Get the kids from the 'sitters. It's exciting, but it still may not be the future of cricket.

I'm talking about Ajantha Mendis, the man who took India apart like they were a birthday cake. This will fall on deaf ears though, because I told people not to get too excited before, and people ignored me.

Yes last night was amazing. Yes we have never seen anything quite like this young man. And yes, the best players of spin in the world just got dissected. But, yet again in capitals for effect, HE IS A MYSTERY SPINNER. Mystery Spinners are unplayable when they first get on the scene.

Eventually they get worked out, then the only ones who stay around are the ones who are just good bowlers. Last night was the first time India had faced him, and they went him, even though they had no idea what he was doing.

He won, they lost.

What happens when all of his deliveries are worked out, when he is no longer a freak show? Well then he will need to just be a good bowler. He may be, but don't think in three years time he will be taking six wicket hauls in one day games.

Let's just sit back. So far he has not played against sides more than a couple of times. There has been no time to work him out. His domestic record is extraordinary, but it was in the second division of Sri Lanka's first class system, which would be the equivalent of grade cricket in Australia.

So far he is doing everything right, and he is exciting, sexy, and doesn't look like he throws, so it's all good. Let's just see if he still doing this sort of stuff in seven years like Warne, Murali and Kumble did. Ask John Gleeson or Jack Iverson what happened once people worked them out.

For every Murali and Clarrie Grimmet, there is a bunch of guys with a card trick or three that get wickets but they don't end up the future of the sport. So let the kid bowl, and stop making him out to be the messiah. He's not even the best spinner in his country yet.

I've watched the video, I've got the woody, the kid is amazing, but once he can be picked he won't be anywhere near as unplayable as last night. There is even a chance last night will be the highlight in his whole career. 6/13 in a final is a pretty good highlight. So lets just soak up the fact a young kid gutted India, and hope he continues to bowl this well.

July 7 - A Spike Lee Joint, "Paul Adams"

In When We Were Kings, Spike Lee talks about how kids these days don't know anything about recent history. I think he is right.

Paul Adams was the frog in a blender, or a midget wearing a bunny suit trying to fling its head at you with a shoulder jerk so savage that it could kill the average ostrich. Everyone remembers that.

Not everyone remembers that batsmen had all sorts of problems playing him when he first came on the scene. At first it was just the action; batsmen couldn't work out where the hell the ball was coming from.

Then when they worked that out, they still had to deal with his wrong 'un, which no one could pick. The Australians picked up that when he bowled his wrong 'un, he flighted it, and when he bowled his stock leggie, he darted it. From there, almost everyone in world cricket worked him out.

In his first year of One Day cricket he took 12 wickets at 19 from seven matches. For the rest of his career he took 17 wickets at 34 from 17 matches. I personally believe Paul Adams was a good bowler, but once he was no longer a mystery South Africa got rid of him. Oh and Paul Adams played five Tests against India. Five matches, 23 wickets at 23 with a best of 6/55.

This record was in 96/97, before he was understood, which explains why he is the only wrist spinner of recent times with a really great record against India.

July 8 - John Stern mentions Bryce McGain

You may not know who John Stern is. He is the editor of The Wisden Cricketer, the magazine ballsy enough to recognise the Balls. At the time I figured the boy who gets the coffees was browsing internet porn one day and found us. Now I see it may have been someone far higher up the tree.

The big boss man. In his article, Mr Stern says, and I quote for effect; "Australia will endeavour to replace Warne - and the newly retired Stuart MacGill - as best they can with Beau Casson or Bryce McGain or whoever, but it's a very tough ask".

See how he put Bryce before whoever, not behind.

Where would a man like John Stern, who usually writes about Kolpaks, Giles Clark and the ICC, find out about Bryce McGain? Need you look further than the blog you are currently reading? Mr Stern has gone even further though; he is actually trying to become a cricket blogger. It's starting to get a bit creepy actually.

I will keep you further updated on John Stern, and if he mentions Natalie Portman, I am getting out a restraining order before he wears my skin as an after dinner jacket.

July 10 - Strauss thinks first slip is more important than second kid

The Wing Commander Andrew Strauss believes in duty. His country, not the one of his birth, but the one of his birth as a Test cricketer, has given him something only a few thousand people have ever received; a Test cap. His wife, not Marcus Trescothick's wife, has given him a child, something that practically every second man in the world has.

No contest. Test cap comes first. After all it's not his first child; that generally only happens once. His wife will have to do the hard yards on her own, for once, not like all those other lazy pregnant women whose husbands and partners do all the hard work while they lay on their back.
What is needed by the English team is child planning. Conception should be part of the Future Tours program. You can't have WAGs giving birth whenever they feel like it;

surely there is a contract that can be signed? And what about pre-Test inducements should the worst happen, and the little bugger is to come out during an important time.

It's not too late to get her to pop it out now, just to make sure there are no distractions. There are varying opinions in the cricket world on the baby debate.

Jeremy Snape wrote in his book "How to Win the English and Proper Way Using Kinetics and Teleporting"*: "Children are important for team bonding. If a star player's wife is due to give birth, all the players should be present at the birth, and key members of the team should be trained as midwives for the occasion".

An excerpt from Steve Waugh's book "I'd Smack my Mother for a Test Win"*: "Players' wives have to be of tough stuff, and henceforth can pop out a young 'un without help of a man, in dusty or bouncy conditions".

And Peter Roebuck once remarked in "How to Bring up South African Cricketers"*: "the problem with kids is they have no discipline, they always do things to get you angry, so if they are born at an inconvenient time, smack them".

I will say this to any future cricketers who may have this same conundrum: you want to gauge your decision from your wife's expression when you first broach the subject.

*Books may not exist, and all quotes may have been falsified, sorry Judge.

July 16 - The Dark Knight – pitch report

If you wanna see Batman, and know nothing about the film when you do, this may not be the page to be reading. It has mild plot spoilers, and if you haven't seen the film it may not make any sense at all. Although, if you haven't seen it by now, why the hell not?

The Dark Knight starts off with the Joker, who resembles what I hope Günter (Andre Nel's alter ego) would look like, having a little moment.

Then there is a bit of Batman, who is like Freddie Flintoff, really cool, but a lot of damage just below the mask. Scarecrow is there for a second, but like Asif, he disappears quickly. The batman meets up with his ex, Rachel Dawes, who looks a bit like Nathan Bracken, and some dude named Harvey Dent. Dent's a little Jacob Oram, if you get my drift. Every now and then we see Lt Gordon, who gets the job done, but is pretty boring, like Mike Hussey. There are mob bosses, one who reminds me of Graeme Smith, and a bank manager who shares similar traits with Mahela.

Günter gets off to a flier, Freddie Flintoff thinks he has him reigned in, especially with a few short ones, but Günter is two steps ahead. Jacob Oram takes over the attack for a while, he goes for line and length, it doesn't work and Bracken has plenty of advice for everyone. M Hussey comes into the attack, but that doesn't end well and Freddie Flintoff has come to come back on.

While this is happening Jacob Oram forgets about bowling and goes and puts his pads on. Mahela and Smithy are pretty much ignored. Predictably things go to shit, Günter is way crazier than Freddie Flintoff could ever understand, Freddie Flintoff is in love with Bracken who is in love with Oram (still the bowling one), M Hussey runs into mischief and Graeme Smith does an amazing imitation of Eric Roberts.

Eventually Freddie Flintoff has to get fit. Jacob puts his pads on. And Günter is one crazy motherfucker.

Best game I've seen this year. Günter plays a blinder in his retirement year. Worth going to all five days.

July 18 - Eyelids is in

Fuck me with a soldering iron. How can this be? Already the comments are coming through. "I can't believe Eyelids is playing a fucking Test" screams Miriam. "You're kidding, he isn't going to be playing for Victoria any more" PK says with shock.

They are all talking about DARREN "EYELIDS" PATTINSON, Victoria's newest English Test cricketer. A very reliable source told me that he is playing for the right county, which is hilarious, because over here he played for the wrong state. But who cares; a Victorian is playing Test cricket.

Dandenong is on the map (although, that probably isn't a good thing). Things to watch out for: his eyelids, the flappers, as he comes in to the crease. His heavy balls, Geoff Miller's words not mine. Decent pace, with a touch of movement.

Eyelids is a manly outdoorsy sort of chap, as most roofers tend to be, but, they tell me, with a heart of gold. And he is playing for England. This is the most exciting thing to happen to mankind since Lyle Lovett hooked Julia. Six months ago he couldn't get a game for Victoria.

Now with 11 first class games, mostly in county cricket, he is in the team ahead of Chris Tremlett, Simon Jones, Matthew Hoggard, Steve Harmison, and Sajid Mahmood.

Fuck me.

Geoff Miller loves Eyelid's heavy balls.

July 18 - Eyelids, a Cricket With Balls prophecy

I have been searching all my old posts and note books for information on Darren Pattinson. I found this first, because I wanted to. It was written on the 23rd of April. "Eyelids also made a stoic 33-odd, so this is a very good start for the man, who I presume will play for England within the next four months." This may be the seventh mention of this quote, sorry.

I really am not an expert on him in real terms (nor am I some sort of cricket soothsayer); I have only seen him bowl maybe five times. This is five more times than anyone in the Sky commentary box from the sound of it. I also found this: "He is a chesty front on sort of bowler, who can bowl into the 140s down breeze on a windy day and seams the ball around a bit".

And this: "He doesn't look like a superstar, but the man gets wickets quite often, perhaps by making the batsman confused at the man running in with his eyes shut".

During my year following the Bushrangers, this is the most I ever mentioned him on the Lone Bushrangers Fan blog (statecricket.com): "This is the most I've seen of Darren Pattinson, and he worries me, not as a bowler, as a bowler I like him, but on the way in to the wicket he seems to almost close his eyes, I'm afraid he'll do himself a mischief".

That is the day I crowned him Eyelids. In conclusion, he is front on, quick enough, ex roof tiler, Dandenong boy, moves the ball, closes his eyes, takes wickets and is a Victorian. Oh, and I forgot to mention, his inclusion is sure to piss off a bunch of English supporters and surprise a whole lot more. So it's a good inclusion for everyone.

July 19 - Darren Pattinson under the microscope

Pattinson's first bowling figures were 30 overs, 2 Maidens, 2 Wickets for 95 runs. It looked far worse.

It has to be said that so far Eyelids has looked as dangerous as Bambi. Perhaps I'm being unfair to Bambi. But a point needs to be made. He does not look like a Test match bowler today. You could argue nerves; a flat pitch and an extremely disciplined South African line up haven't helped.

This is the slowest I have ever seen him bowl, and by far the most erratic. At this pace, you can't afford to be erratic. On paper he has bowled as well as Broad, and he probably has on the field as well, but Broad is a foetus. Take one look at Pattinson's eyes, if you can, and they show a man of many years.

He is lucky if he bowls three testing balls a spell, and Vaughan clearly does not see anything he likes. Every spell he bowls the pressure is lifted, and he does not have the weaponry to endanger set batsman on this kind of pitch. Right now you'd argue this is going to be Eyelids' only Test.

And he is bowling like he has already accepted it.

July 23 - My application

The Blackcaps are looking for a new coach, as John Bracewell is taking a more important job. So here is my application.

My name is Uncle Jrod, and I hereby apply for the full time position of Black Caps coach. I have looked at your seven page proposal and your goal of being ranked number one or two by 2011, and I know I am the man for the job as I have no grip on reality either.

KPIs.
New Zealand need to improve all their key performance indicators. Namely, they need more wickets and more runs. I will assist in this process.

BLUE SKY THINK TANKS
Meetings between myself, and other individuals who have the courage, creativity and clarity to find new ways for the Black Caps to go forward, and dare I say it, conquer the world.

MY WAR STORY
Over the years I have had many major cricketing moments, but the one that suits me best as Black Caps coach was when I got hit 17 times on the body by someone everyone called Killer (not just because his surname was Kilpatrick), and I may have foolishly called an Ox, due to his large nature. I ended up making 27 runs. Meaning I averaged 1.58 runs to every blow. Surely that makes me over-qualified to coach New Zealand.

WEB 2.0 INITIATIVES
All players to regularly blog, Facebook and come up with their own MySpace page, I love that retro stuff. This is to allow fans to connect with the players and have a meshing of the minds, avatars and souls. We call it synergy.

DIVERSITY AWARENESS SESSIONS
A three day intense camp in which all players will have to try to bowl the carrom ball, and to study the techniques of Malinga and Chanderpaul.

MY INTEGRATED SOLUTION 10 POINT FRAMEWORK

1. Move the top 20 players to Bangladesh. New Zealand doesn't want you, and Bangladesh would love to see real cricketers from time to time. It doesn't have to be full time, just ten months a year. It's nice to feel appreciated.
2. Jacob Oram will be fed a diet of short deliveries. Nothing else, no medium pacers or spinners, just quicks and ball machines at his curly bonce. Also, Ian Smith will be banned from pumping him up.
3. No more "middle players". Players will be picked if they are young and talented, or if they are proven; nothing in between. No spinners who become openers, or any of that nonsense. A mix of youth and experience is clichéd as a motherfucker, but it works.
4. The ICL can kiss my arse, Shane Bond is a New Zealand cricketer, and he plays for us. If Lalit Modi wants to stop him playing, he can kidnap him.
5. Stephen Fleming can retire whenever he wants, but hopefully not before we find a number three to replace him. He can wait ten years, can't he?

6. Arseholes. It's all well and good to be arseholes against minnows and Sri Lanka, but you used to be arseholes against Australia, and that was grand.
7. Get an Australian coach, like me. We are the cat's pyjamas; for proof see Greg Chappell, Jamie Siddons and Geoff Lawson.
8. Brothers, New Zealand teams always play better with brothers, and no, not the Marshall brothers; they're rubbish. Isn't there a Nathan that matches Brendon?
9. Picking players who will win cricket matches, and not those who are less likely to lose them, is a good start. If we can't win Test matches we can sure as hell make people want to watch us.
10. Every team needs a drunkard, and if Warnie and Freddie have taught us anything, it's that they are the key ingredient to build your team around. How is young Jesse's hand doing?

NEXT STEPS

Test selection

How – New Zealand with a real opener.
Flynn – He's not a middle order batsman, but the boy has balls, send him to the top.
Fleming – My only other option was Two-Meter Peter Fulton, and that's not really an option.
Taylor – It's his.
Ryder – Not worried about fitness or consumption of alcohol, just batsmanship.
McCullum – The Prince.
Oram – Probably needs a haircut.
Vettori – As a batting captain and part time bowler.
Patel – Your best spinner should play, not be a tourist.
Bond – Remember him?
Martin – Has a bit in him.
12th man – McCullum, N – got to fit a brother in.

Assistant Coach: sportsfreak.co.nz. You need a hard-arse bagman as assistant coach and he will be my key enabler. He is also here for cultural differences between me and the players.

Media Manager: Sportreview.net.nz. He can handle the incoming rubbish while keeping me out of the loop.

Team Portrait: cricketactionart.blogspot.com. Airbrush required to reconstruct the look of New Zealand.

Cricket Existentionalist: OutsidetheLine.typepad.com. It's about cricket, or is it? Will also help with corporate visions, or so it seems.

Embedded Journalist: Crucket.co.nz. Everyone needs good press, and outsourcing is the best way.

July 28 - Watching the English, a guide for the Jrod

Miriam put together this helpful guide for Jrod's move to London.

The Jrod is, as we speak, in midair making his way over to this green and pleasant land. While he is over here I expect he will go to watch some live cricket. Balls fans, what does he need to know? I start you off with some suggestions.

1. However hot the day might seem, always, always take a jumper and an umbrella
2. However cold the day might seem, always, always take a hat, sunglasses and suncream.
3. You are still allowed to take alcohol into Lord's, and you can maximise the units of alcohol by taking wine not beer.
4. There is no cashpoint near the Oval, and there isn't really anywhere to get picnic food either, unless it's a Saturday in which case the farmers' market is open.
5. Don't go to the first beer stall; go to the second.
6. The Oval scoreboard will make you cry with frustration.
7. You will get frisked with a metal detector on the way in to big matches. Therefore, it's probably best to leave the remote control sex toy at home.
8. A counselling course is required before you undergo the trauma of paying for a pint of Pimms.
9. At Test matches, you will be tempted to change energy supplier by attractive blonde sirens. Resist.
10. Whatever they might say on the tannoy at Lord's, St John's Wood Tube is not too busy for going home.
11. Never rely on being able to watch cricket in any particular pub. It will most probably be bumped if anything - anything - else is on.
12. The beer sold at the grounds is shocking.
13. If you are repeatedly buying multiple pints, hang on to the cardboard carrying thing because they sometimes run out of them by the end of the day.
14. Tickets for county games are very expensive compared with Australian state games.

July 29 - The backlift of Rikki Clarke

When I first arrived in England one of the first things I saw was a Pro40 game, which is England's third domestic limited overs competition.

There are many things I could tell you about England. It is insanely hot here. And they have a lot of fried chicken. But England is summed up by one thing.

Rikki Clarke's backlift.

I don't believe anyone could have a backlift like it and not be English. It looks like a gay actor's interpretation of Graham Gooch's backlift. Stiff, proper and camp. Like a cup of tea, or Prince Charles. Or Prince Charles drinking a cup of tea, but thinking of a pint of beer.

Clarke seems to make some runs in spite of his backlift handicap, although he does seem to be late on every attacking shot he plays. Apparently Clarke played Test cricket once. I think it is good he doesn't play anymore, as children imitate Test cricketers, and he could start a pandemic of weird backlifts.

I say all this because I saw Rikki Clarke make runs. The commentators seemed rather excited by it. I was not.

August 1 - He made 200 runs and they undressed accordingly

Unfortunately due to cable TV rights I couldn't see the series between India and Sri Lanka, but Sehwag still shone through.

It wasn't that long ago that Sehwag was wandering the desert. Unwanted by his people and most major sponsors. He was cast aside for men with lusher hair and more athletic physiques. Perth was his Easter-type cave. Now he is ballsier, harder, stronger, balder and better than ever before. Like a peacock rubbed in Vaseline.

In his new Godlike form he is trying to make sure that when great Indian batsman are mentioned, VVS, Dravid and Ganguly have to line up behind the bald prophet for their props. His latest miracle was 200 out of 330.

Making half the runs of your team is phenomenal. But Sehwag didn't even bother with that. The little fella was one of three Indians to get beyond seven runs. Mendis continues his modern magic tricks, each more mysterious and evil than the last. Sehwag uses brutal force to dispel the spells. Like an angry fat man swatting away flies from a burger.

The man is on top of the mountain at the moment. Every time Sehwag hits a four, an angel loses its virginity.

And let us hope that angels continue to be bad little girls for some time yet.

August 3 - Vaughan is about to be fired, I s'pose

I and only a few million others see the writing on the wall.

Big news is about to break over here. Michael Vaughan, former superstar batsman and decent captain, but current bum of the month, is about to get the arse. I have this on no real authority other than a gut feeling, and a slight stirring downstairs.

This can mean only one thing: Kingcricket.co.uk's Own Rob Key will come in at number three and captain England. I know that is a lot of what-ifs, but I figured if you throw enough shit against a wall some of it is bound to stick. Not that Rob Key is shit, well not completely shit.

Vaughan should be fired, but there are many other questions: will England have the balls to make the tough call? Which formerly tried cricketer will they bring in to replace him? Does Wing Commander Strauss want to replace him? Should KP smile less?

England also has two soft-cock options available to them. Vaughan slides down the order, and they manufacture a number three out of Bell. Or they pray to WG Grace that Vaughan gets his mojo back for next year's Ashes.

Because as we all know, the Ashes are all that matters; losses to India, Sri Lanka and South Africa mean very little to the Brits. Remember when they won the 2005 Ashes? Memories, like the rest of the lyrics in that song go. Is it too late to bring back Fletcher, Harmison, Hoggard, Giles, and co for the next Ashes?

August 4 – Captain KP?

England seemed hell-bent on taking KP as captain, so I looked at it objectively.

Random musings on the nation builder.

He is not English. This is not the NBA (marquee players don't have to be given the job). Is there really a tactical brain in there? He is South African. You shouldn't pick the man most likely to play in both squads, pick the best man in each squad.

He has hardly been a team player in the past when it comes to his batting position. "It's your nation". Which KP will captain, the flamboyant swiper, or the dour lost boy? Will he be able to talk about himself in the third person? Has he ever captained a cricket team before? Arrogant prick?

If he couldn't play cricket, would he be let into the longroom? What actual captaincy qualities has ever shown? Too entertaining? Will he be able to get into a rumour involving another player's wife? Remember when he had sore ribs and went home? Will he be able to take the pressure of the vicious strikes the media will inflict on him?

Is he the poor man's Beckham?

August 4 - KP, now it's your nation

England bite the bullet and pick KP as captain.

England has swiftly appointed KP as its commander in chief. Rob Key and Tim Ambrose were hardly discussed. This is now KP's team. So it needs some remodelling.

Freddie will have to get that brown hair spot fixed.
Strauss will need a haircut that public schools don't sanction.
Cook will need to paint his nails to match his eyeliner.
Sidebottom may get dropped.
Collingwood won't be allowed to wear Hawaiian shirts on tour anymore.
Ambrose, total makeover.
Bell, number one all over, and more bracelets.
Anderson will be made vice captain.
And Monty, team mascot.

August 14 - Fuck the Ashes, bring on the Saffas

Right now I couldn't give a rat's arse about the Ashes. Because Australia have a home series against the South Africans to win. So KP, all the English press and anyone else who thinks there is only one series in the world can kiss my arse. If we lose to South Africa at home, 2000 and 5 will feel like a fucking good time to be alive.

Australia will no longer be the world's best team, and it's been a long time since I have had to deal with that reality. I know they aren't very good. I have mentioned this robustly. But neither is any other side in the world.

South Africa still have a shaky top seven, and their bowlers didn't impress in England. India look the real deal at times, and look like Walter Matthau and Jack Lemmon at others. Sri Lanka got smoked in Australia, and then looked asleep against the Windies, but are currently riding the Mendis steam train of love. England just lost to South Africa at home, so I am wasting keystrokes here.

If Australia can stay number one through their transition stage, we may see another decade of them on top. But if South Africa beat them at home, well, my my, my reality matrix will be seriously fucked up.

Down will become up, Orwellian mathematics will be applied, healthy food will taste good, reality TV will make sense, and Natalie Portman will lose her appeal. I am sorry South Africa, I am not ready for that life change right now, so for the good of my mental health you will have to lose.

You know, like you always do against Australia.

August 20 - Cricket With Balls does it again, literally

David Hussey, in the Australian side. Check. Uncle Jrod in the Wisden cricketer. Check. Natalie Portman nude in a film that mentions cricket. Check.

And now we have got McGain a ticket to India. An "Australia A" gig, but a real life e-ticket on a plane to play cricket in India with the words Australia on his hat. Pat yourself on the back readers.

McGain finds himself in a "bowl off" with "talk about me" Jason Krejza and "The Young & the Restless" Beau Casson. The world seems a less cold place today. The flowers are blooming. The kids are smiling. And an Ageing Experienced Victorian Warrior gets a step closer to glory.

Glory that is rightfully his. Glory that no man, woman, child, God or alien would dare to stop him from. Bryce, the chickens are coming home to roost dude.

I can only take you so far Bryce, I got you a ticket, but only you can get the wickets.

August 25 - Is this a mint I see before me?

Marcus Trescothick releases a book in which he admits to ball tampering, and it won awards; who says cheats never prosper?

We now know that Marcus Trescothick is one horrendous cheat. Because he told us, and look at his eyes (photo could not be reproduced in the book as his evil blue eyes would scare the kiddies).

If you want to know the full story, buy his book Coming Over Me (actually titled Coming Back to Me). Less than a year after he cheated, his career was over because of depression (not true, it was the Ashes 2001 he admitted to cheating in, but truth never gets in the way). Because some men are made to be cheats, and then there is Marcus.

Marcus has been chased by the ghost of Banquo ever since. Yes I'm using Shakespeare, but try to follow. Macbeth ordered Banquo (2005 Ashes) and his son Fleance (future Ashes) killed. Only Banquo was killed, Fleance survived. When Banquo was killed, he came back to Macbeth in ghost form, and tormented the fucker for his actions.

In conclusion: the ghost of cheating at the 2005 Ashes has stalked Marcus ever since, and that is why he is depressed. Also Lady Macbeth was hard work.

So karma (or the ghost) got the better of this fresh mouthed fucker. The Australian players lost an Ashes, got fired up, smoked England in the next series while Marcus sat at home and fought with the black dog. A 30-year-old cricketer was lost to the game, England now look as dodgy as Pakistan at their foulest and Australia has all the necessary motivation to win next year's Ashes.

And Marcus has sold quite a few copies of his book.

August 27 - Goodbye Mushie

Mushtaq Ahmed quits county cricket.

The great little man has left the building. Grand Master Mushtaq has quit Sussex and we will never see that double arm twirl again. Mushtaq was more than a bowler to me: he was leg spin. I even have the unnecessary double arm twirl in my action.

While the whole world was going crazy over Warne, I was a Mushie fan. In Melbourne, that never went down that well. Mushie bounced in, and he was magical, like a leprechaun on ice. Warne was the leg spinner you liked if you knew nothing about leg spinning. Mushie was the leg spinner's leggie, a performance artist who relied on enough leg spin to beat the bat without being ridiculous about it.

He was a pure leg spinner. His weapon was the wrong 'un, and what a weapon it was; it didn't spin back in at the stumps, it honed in on them like a heat-seeking missile. His toppie was so simple you could almost discount it as a great ball, which is why it was so good. Everyone waited for the wrong 'un to destroy them, but more often than not the toppie got them first.

His leggies may not have spun sideways, but they span, they bounced, and they fizzed, oh how they fizzed. Quite often the most simple of cut shots seemed impossible as Mushie would drag you into the position he wanted, and then plan your demise. He was not a one ball wicket taker; he could plan a batsman out for several overs until he had them just where he wanted them.

At the '92 World Cup he showed that spinners weren't just window dressing in One Day matches; they could be kings. And he was king in that World Cup. Over the years Pakistan politics, Saqlain's doosra, and old age meant that his genius was not shown on the world stage anywhere near enough. Instead he found himself embraced in county cricket.

There his legend actually grew, as he took Sussex and put them on his shoulders. Even from Melbourne I would follow Mushie at Sussex, and just marvel at the sheer weight of wickets the little man with the huge heart would take. Chris Adams, Sussex's captain, gushed about Mushie as a cricketer, but he even went a step further. "He is simply a great man".

One of the things I wanted to do when I first got to London was watch Mushie one last time, and selfishly, I am angry that those little knees of his couldn't keep him out long enough for me to see one last spell of magic. His body knew it was time to leave.

To me he was more than a bowler. He was a hero, an idol, a God, and I am heartbroken to see him go.

Thanks for the magic, Mushie.

August 28 - Chaminda the small wonderhorse

You have to respect Chaminda Vaas. Not just on his 400 wickets in One Day cricket. But on knowing where his place is in the world. He knows he isn't Wasim Akram. But only three others have taken 400 wickets. And he is still humble. "There were a lot of guys more talented than me, my game was limited but I worked harder. Nothing comes easy to you, you have got to make the most of your talent".

These days other cricketers make a few hundreds or take a big haul or two and you'd think they were Elvis. Sri Lanka grows humble cricketers who perform over and over again, while bigger name players from other countries squander away their talent like horny sailors.

Yuvraj Singh was Vaas' 400th. Life can be poetic. Vaas wouldn't make comments like this though; too good a bloke.

If I took 400 One Day wickets I would be running around the stadium naked covered in eagle feathers drunk on seven bottles of Canadian Club until I collapsed.

There have been times when Vaas has been the best One Day bowler in the world, statistically and realistically. Like the 2000 and 3 World Cup. The man is a worker, a miniature Clydesdale, and few have represented Sri Lanka better in the history of cricket. Cricket With Balls salutes the man.

August 31 - South Africa, made of butter?

After KP took over England started to win, dead rubber Tests and One Dayers.

It's easy to bag a team out of form. So let me bag South Africa for a moment. Graeme Smith is the number one rated One Day batsman in the world. He is out injured. Let us look at the rest of the One Day batsmen South Africa have.

Gibbs – well past his best. Just holding on to his position, and is probably there as much because the rest of the batsmen are boring. Should be pensioned off.
Amla - Looked the goods yesterday, but he needs to bat with someone who has after burners, not Jacques Kallis like yesterday. A possible anchor man if they have the artillery around him.
Kallis – looking old and finished right at the moment. Hard to knock someone with his record, but this tour of England is looking horrible. And in the World Cup Ponting was hoping to keep him at the crease if you remember. Gone?

deVilliers – Hard to put a marker on him. Has the youth and skill to be a batsman, but seems soft under pressure. Looks like a front-runner and is yet to convince me. Ten year player, or a ten year Kolpak player.

Duminy – Haven't seen much of him, but does make some runs. Looks like another flat track, front running South African batsman, which is their forte. Has the right colour to have a long career, but is he any good?

Boucher – Always been South Africa's best batsman in a scrap. Has more fight then the rest of the team combined. But at six? That is a proper batting slot. If he is at six, what sort of batting does South Africa have?

Morkel – Sure he can hit, I can attest to that after watching a six go flying over my head, but you wouldn't say there is a lot of thinking going on up there. When the going is tough, can he put in something other than a sloggers innings?

England does have a good bowling line up, but this is a batting line up made of butter: don't leave it out in the sun too long.

The bowlers.

Steyn – Where is Dale Steyn? He clearly never turned up to England.

Ntini – He is a One Day disaster case. Should not be playing One Day cricket.

(Supervillain) Morne Morkel – Bowls well, always looks dangerous, but never cuts a swathe through a line up.

Kallis – Still Kallis.

(Baby Face) Albie Morkel – Is a pretty handy One Day bowler, has a great yorker, and you wonder why others get the death overs.

Botha – Has an action that would make Murali cry. But is hard to get away, even if he can't get wickets.

Right at the moment this does not look like the recent top ranked One Day side. There are holes everywhere in this line up. England, who are up, are slapping them all over the place. South Africa always play great cricket against average sides, but how many times do they struggle against good teams in form?

September 4 - NO, No , No NO, No no n ono n o non ono

Cricket With Balls' own Nice Bryce McGain injures himself on his Australian A tour of India.

This cannot be happening. Bryce is injured. His shoulder. It no worky. His fucking bowling shoulder.

Just when my Beau Casson voodoo doll works, Beau Casson's mum uses a spell she saw on Passions and Bryce is fucked. He didn't bowl at all today, which is a shame as the India "A" tail fell apart. Lots of cheap wickets were there to be had while Beau was getting his groin touched by men.

Why is this happening to me, um, Bryce? It is an actual tragedy, not like Princess Di dying or Steve Irwin chestfucking a stinger, but a real life tragedy. This is horrible. This is by far the worst thing to ever happen, ever. The world seems like a cold and dark place.

Of all the rainy days and false starts that cricket has given us there has never been a depression like this just sweep the cricket world in one foul swoop of darkness and the sudden chest pressing of heartache and loss that no one person should ever have to live through, like outliving your children or learning that Santa Claus is a paedophile which are not even apt metaphors as this is far worse than even having to eat your own testicles covered in your own faeces does which still doesn't compare to this this this horrible moment in human history the holocaust of cricket moments in fact some may say worse than the holocaust it makes the tsunami look like a ripple and people will be saying "I remember where I was when Bryce got hurt" and they will cry and wail and we can only hope that one day the world will make sense again and that the aliens do in fact have a plan for us where hurting someone as pure and good as Bryce makes sense.

Of course on the plus side I now know my voodoo doll works. I was a bit worried when it was reported that Beau had injured his hamstring, because I knew I wasn't poking there.

September 12 - Fishing for the truth

In possibly the most un-Australian moment in Australian cricket history, Andrew Symonds was sent home from a One Day series against Bangladesh because he missed a meeting he was not aware of because he was fishing.

I knew there was something fishy about the whole barramundigate (Symonds's fishing adventure). Turns out the story is all sorts of bullshit.

The fishing has nothing/very little to do with it, as it seems like the boys are having a few issues with each other before Darwin. Apparently Michael Clarke and Symonds had a little falling out in the Windies, and they haven't slept with each other since. Symonds used to be loved by the boys for being un-Probotic, you know, human.

Now that has all changed; Pup is already putting his mark on the team, and drinking and fishing are not allowed. Pup probably thought telling Symonds off would fire him up for India, but instead it has landed the Australians with Shane Watson. I have already stated my thoughts on this. I am less than pleased.

You can't talk a guy up because he is relaxed, and then shunt him off for the same reason. This may be the first time in history Australian players have had a bad team experience in a bar. They should have stuck to drinking on planes.

September 12 - Hallelujah

Bryce McGain got picked for the Australian squad in India.

We're free at last, we're free at last, thank the aliens almighty, we are free at last.

Today birds are smiling, bees are singing, and the children, oh the children, they have never seen so much joy. They are glowing in a radiation of pure happiness and they are positively gay. I feel like a teenage boy who has just pressed pause while watching Basic Instinct for the first time.

This is like in that scene where Lassie finds the young boy down the well and resuscitates him while the townsfolk are all paralysed from syphilis. Remember when man walked on the moon? Remember when you first saw Natalie Portman? Remember when that first girl or boy touched you down there? This is like that moment only with ten times more awesomeness.

It's like seeing Godzilla in real life, or meeting an alien for a cup of tea. It's as good as: Bambi's mum coming back to life. Dubya Bush being disembowelled in a horrible rodeo accident. Finding out a rich relative you hate has died and because of a typo in the will you get it all. Old Yeller wasn't really dead, and was planning on having you as its owner.

This is life, a pure shot of life injected straight into your hardened heart. This is a sunny day in a can.

Viva la revolution, Viva la Bryce.

So wherever you are take a moment to soak in the glory that is Bryce getting picked for Australia. Miracles do happen.

Remember, blogs can come true.

September 13 - Jesse is back

One of Cricket With Balls' favourite cricketers is back, and now he is a Test player. Like everyone in the cricket world I was appalled and pissing myself when Jesse Ryder lost his fight with a toilet window.

Things haven't been the same since Jesse left us. Food hasn't tasted as fatty. Tequila hasn't been consumed at Olympic standards. And no other player has had a comedic fall from grace since then. Sure Gibbs went for a drive on the sauce, and Symonds went fishing, but it's hardly the same.

Ryder is to be touring Bangladesh, so he even gets a chance to start with a Bradman-style average. There is some bad news though. The man, affectionately known as

Badonkadonk Ryder, has vowed not to touch the booze for the whole time he is in Bangladesh.

The only question is now, with drinking out of the question, how Jesse will fuck up his tour of Bangladesh?

September 16 - Mr Sutherland, can we have our Australian cricket team back?

My response to the Andrew Symonds debacle.

An open letter to Australia's Chief Administracrat, and a Facebook group to boot.

Excuse me Mr Sutherland, sorry to interrupt your tastily arranged lunch, but we need to talk. We have been watching cricket for a long time, and we used to love watching the Australian cricket team. Alas, now we are watching some sick Probot (professional robot cricketer) circus. Somehow you have infected them all with this new-found "professionalism" and we don't like it.

It sickens us. We want the Australian team to represent Australia, not some multi-national boardroom. Our cricketers should be: Rough. Interesting. Flawed. Fishermen. Fighters. Drunkards. Moustached. Chubby. Badly attired. Cheats. Hairy. Sledgers. Angry.

As long as our cricketers don't hit women, molest small children or have sex with dogs, we really don't care what they do when they are not kicking other countries' arses. Don't pick cricketers based on who Weetbix would approve, who looks better in a suit or based on Peter Roebuck's latest column about the decline of some make-believe notion of the spirit of cricket.

Pick them on skill, guts, and determination. If you want to be able to sell boxes of salted snacks, cars or diarrhoea medicine, surely a winning team with a personality will sell more than a team of perfectly behaved losers. So let the boys play cricket, you know, their job.

We will only ask nicely once.

September 17 - Hard to find a good man

New Zealand Cricket is currently courting several men as head coach. None of them are John Bracewell, and New Zealand Cricket seemed to really like John Bracewell. No one is sure why; all of the NZC's friends thought John Bracewell was an arse. An actual arse, but New Zealand Cricket was smitten.

So when Bracewell decided to see other people, NZC had to start dating again. It wanted someone arrogant, full of themselves, and well thought of. So they pretty much went to Australia and South Africa. South Africa threw up shady individuals, and even though NZC liked the mystery, when Ford asked them to hold a brown paper bag but told them "for fuck's sake don't look in the bag", they decided he could be a bit too mysterious.

Then they looked back at Australia. Vettori told them he had found the perfect guy for them while back packing in India. He was stoic, determined, intelligent, and used to coaching a team of all rounders with no real top order. Unfortunately Ship decided to stay with Victoria, as their players are far less likely to become Kolpaks or play in the ICL.

Then Brendon chipped in, he met a bloke while he was at a rave in Goa. The guy was quiet, but he knew how to deal with talent. Also, he let Brendan talk and talk. Problem was he was already dealing with an international side in New South Wales, and the drop off in talent could be an issue for him.

Frustrated with all these false starts, and unfulfilled desires, someone at NZC suggested stealing someone else's man. So NZC looked around world cricket for someone who could coach, that narrowed it down, and someone who was disillusioned with his team. This lead them to another South African, sure he was taken, but he didn't seem that happy with his current team, and it's not like he has to come over straight away, NZC is still having some goodbye sessions with Braces.

But all this flirting, courting, and waiting is pointless anyway. Just fling a dart at a board and pick your next loser. Time get on with your life; with your taste in men, the longer you take, the worse you'll end up.

Mr Right doesn't exist.

September 18 - Holy fuckamoly

While I was at the Oval watching Shoaib Ahktar's cameo for Surrey, something wonderful happened.

While I was Shoaib-watching, a real man, the real man, took six wickets for 32 for Middlesex. The real man, as if you didn't know, is Dirty Dirk Nannes. Six wickets for 32, did you hear the moon scream? Wild, animalistic, colonial, aggressive, and pure masculinity.

When Dirty Dirk gets wickets, mountains fall. Pygmies cry. And the world seems right, whole and perverted, like it should do.

For some reason, Shaun Udal, Middlesex's 14th captain this year, brought Dirk on third change. Worcs were bowled out for 122. Had he opened the bowling, like he always should, he would have bowled them out for 32. And taken ten wickets. That is the sort of mood he was in.

I wasn't there, but I am sure at a lunch break he ate a cow, rare, or raw. You haven't seen anything like Dirty Dirk in full flight, and since no one was in Warwickshire today, no one else has either. What I wouldn't have given to watch the big ex-bearded one steam in and take six wickets as men cowered in change rooms and women disrobed in unison.

Instead I saw Shoaib stretch. A lot.

September 22 - Is it racist to call an Asian batsman wristy?

Yesterday I watched the Pro40 playoff between men in green pyjamas and Jason Gillespie. In this game, Vikram Solanki and Moeen Ali had a bit of a partnership. The commentators took this as their cue to say the word wristy in every sentence. When you hear an English commentator say a batsman is wristy, 'tis his way of saying, "he's brown he is".

Lots of batsmen around the world are wristy; it's not just a sub-continental way of playing. You don't even need to be brown to do it. White players have been, and are, wristy. But for some reason white commentators never notice this. Get a brown player in, and even if his wrists are made of lead, he is wristy.

A white player needs Sachin Tendulkar wrists even to be noticed, and even then the white one has great wrist work, whereas a brown player would be wristy.

Bloody racists, every Pommy one of them.

September 25 - Imran, take a bow you alice banded freak

As part of my foray into cricket journalism I found myself at Trent Bridge watching Nottingham try to beat Hampshire for the title.

Earlier in this match I had written off Imran Tahir. In my defence I would like to say that I was completely justified, as he was bowling garbage. Rancid lettuce, stinky tomatoes, fermented mayonnaise, decaying bananas, you know, garbage. Then he bowled a spell that would have given a nun a hot flush, a eunuch a stiffy, and turned a liberal into a gun-toting psychopath, had any of them understood leg spin.

Not understood, dug leg spin, I mean really feel leg spin. The sort of person who teaches his girlfriend leg spin with an apple. If you had a deep emotional and sexual connection with leg spin, Tahir's spell was free hard-core porn with no download limits. Wrong 'uns, flippers, toppies, and sliders were all used, and he took Notts from championship to calamity. 'Twas a beautiful moment.

Graeme Swann had a top spinner so vicious that if it were a cobra he would be dead. Mark Ealham missed a flipper that made Clarrie Grimmett want to come back from the dead, mount Tahir from behind, and then bowl at the other end. Andre Adams didn't even get a chance to get angry as he missed a wrong 'un so delicious you could taste it. If Mark Nicholas were here, he would have judged it Britain's top meal. And Eyelids Pattinson was just not up to the magic as another perfectly placed wrong 'un cannoned into the stumps like a thirsty child jumping into a lake in the desert.

It was like watching a "how to bowl leg spin and fuck people over" video. Once Samit Patel was out, that was it. The genie came out of the bottle wearing high heels, no knickers and a wicked smile. Tahir excited me more in fours overs than Danish Kaneria has in his whole career.

This spell was the equivalent of heroin for an addict, or a willing 12-year-old boy for a priest. Imran, if I had Natalie Portman's number I would seriously consider giving it to you right now.

September 26 - Just fix it

The McGain shoulder is still not working. This hurts me, deeply. He is still yet to bowl a delivery on this tour, and what is it, like two days old? The first Test is only so far away. Tim Neilson isn't worried, but he is the man who hired Greg Chappell.

Where is Errol Hooter Allcot when you need him? If he is good enough for Russell - cousin of Martin and Jeff - Crowe, and Shane Warne, then he is almost good enough for Our Bryce.

Hooter can fix anything. One time in Karachi, Warne's arm came off in a nasty orgy incident. He thought his career was over, but Hooter took a tub of Vaseline, bluetack, and a screwdriver and put that shoulder back together.

That is the sort of work Bryce needs.

September 27 - Don't you dare say the "M" word you monkey

Robert Key shocked the cricket world by saying the one word that should never be used. Muppets.

To call a selector, an administracrat, or a pitch inspector a muppet is the single worst word you can use. Call them cock-suckers. Compare them to a dildo. Mention what a massive arse-clown they are. But don't you dare call them muppets. It's offensive, to muppets.

Robert Key was fined 1250 quid for using the "M" word, which for an IPL cricketer is the cash you use to light your cigar with, but for someone on Key's salary it's serious money. I mean other than pie sponsorship deals and Kent, who is going to give him money?

In related news Jim Henson's estate are looking at taking a class action suit out against the ICC and all major cricket boards for defamation of his characters. A lawyer for the estate read a prepared statement. "The muppets are a well loved family entertainment icon. As a brand we would not like them brought down to the standard of any cricket officials. We think this is a gross injustice, and we are looking into the legalities of these continuing incidents at the moment".

October 1 - Bryce's soliloquy redux

Even the ticket to India does not cheer up Bryce's shoulder, and he is set to miss the first Test, although he still thinks he will be fit for the second.

Have you ever lost a loved one?

I don't mean some parent, kid or fellow sibling that you have vague nostalgic affection for. I mean a real loved one, someone who by their very lack of existence leaves a void in your soul, a hole in your heart, a vacancy in your raison d'être, a dissipation of your erection, a pain in your gut so hurtful it feels like a million miniature pit bulls are attacking every part of your insides?

Pain, severe pain.

Pain of a level that getting your foreskin caught in a zipper feels like nothing, getting your foot run over by a station wagon doesn't register, having that first girl tell you she doesn't like you is palatable, losing that special grandparent, you know the one you really like is something you can handle, living a life of such tedium that you fantasise about killing the people you work with is acceptable compared to "this".

The "this" is that Bryce's shoulder is still no good. He is out of the first Test. He may be out of the tour. He may never get to play Test cricket. This shoulder of his, this fucking rebellious limb, is fucking up my universe. It's taking my hope away.

The story of Bryce McGain is supposed to be special. He is supposed to be a prophet for anyone who had a dream and didn't give up.

His age didn't stop him.
His kid didn't stop him.
His job didn't stop him.

The continuing disappointments of life and love didn't stop him. He had a dream that no one else believed in and he was this close. So close he could almost feel how the Baggy Green would feel on his head.

And the fucking shoulder, that cunt of a shoulder, fucked up the whole story, the feel-good story of all time, the story that shows us that dreams can come true, the story that shows us that belief in ourselves can move mountains, the story that shows us that hard work can overcome anything, and that shoulder, that motherfucking prick of a cunt of a shoulder with no sense of history or happy endings just comes in, and it fucks it all up, it shits on Bryce's dream, it shits on the cricket battlers' story of the new millennium, it just reaches into my chest and takes away my heart, and fucks up everything, every fucking little fucken thing, it just came in and it ruined it all, when we were so close, so fucken close to seeing one of us, a working stiff, a family man, a cricket fan, a weekend player make it to where each and every one of us dreams we could, Test cricket, he was our portal, he wasn't some professional athlete who has had his balls licked since he was 12, he was an IT guy who rocked up for his team on a weekend, he wasn't some millionaire whinging about the stress and tireless nature of international cricket, he fucken loved every bit of training, travelling the whole bit of it he was just one of us, he calls himself Joe Average, and now the dream is all fucked up, it might never come back.

He might not ever play Test cricket. It took him 36 years to get this close, and he still might not make it. I can't deal with this.

Today is not a rainy day, today there is no sun.

October 2 - 20.0-1-123-0-6.15-(2nb,0w)

Jason Krejza makes his debut for Australia in a warm up game.

What do numbers mean? To some people the numbers in the title mean nothing. They are just random digits sitting on a blog about a sport that scares or bores them. But for the Off Spinning Pole Krejza, these numbers would have scared the hell out of him.

Now other numbers will start to get to him. First class bowling average of 48. Averaging two first class wickets a game in his career. And tomorrow morning he wakes up, and every paper, blog, and a stone tablet in the world will be baying for his blood.

The Australian papers will be talking about how four quicks is the only way. The Indian papers will be asking if this is the best spinner we have left. The Australian blogs will be in mourning. And the Indian blogs will have peed themselves multiple times.

McGain must be rolling over in his hospital bed. This is not looking pretty, but Jason, they are just numbers, keep up with giving the ball a rip, in the nets.

October 4 - Krazy Krejza Kokaine Kase

Jason Krezja's career goes from bad to worse, as the media cotton on that he once had a positive drug test.

As if the last couple of days have not been hard enough for Jason Krejza, now his sordid past has come out. He once pissed cocaine into a cup. In Sydney. True story.

Apparently he felt his drink was spiked, which is often code for "fuck what if we have a drug test soon?". So he told the officials, they pulled him out of a game, and he tested positive to cocaine (please say it with a wacky Colombian accent). Then in his subsequent tests there was no cocaine.

Drink spiking is a major problem for cricketers. Especially fringe state cricketers. As Cricket Australia's Michael Brown puts it, "I saw a report recently that stated there were around 4,000 reported cases of drink spiking last year ... and higher-profile athletes and celebrities can be targeted".

So in 2000 and 6, what was Jason Krejza, a high profile athlete or a celebrity? Are there random drink spikers just looking for the drinks of Shield players?

Are Daniel Marsh, Michael Klinger and Steve Magoffin in all sorts of trouble? Are doe-eyed young cricketers trained in how to spot a potential Shield doping sex pest? Those questions are hard to answer.

But I will leave you with this one: do you believe him? Brown I mean, not Krejza, I just assume you don't believe him, but do you believe before last week that Krejza was ever high profile? Add this to Krejza's drink driving past and he is pretty much ready to be an Australian cricket legend.

October 6 - Daniel Vettori's fantastical magical tour

New Zealand have flown to Bangladesh. They are going to play cricket there, try and contain your excitement. Daniel Vettori hasn't arrived in Bangladesh though. He has arrived at some wonderfully magic place full of fairy floss, golden nipples and Test match standard cricketers.

A place so special and exciting money does grow on trees, you can buy bottled monkeys, prostitutes give you the first visit for free and Swedish models lick your toes everyday, and twice on Thursdays. This is what Daniel "I've lost his frame of reference" Vettori has said about his special place. "I think most countries who come to Bangladesh know they are in for a difficult time".

He is right, the commute from Dhaka International to the Dhaka Hilton is arduous, and who can be bothered with that after a long flight on Ansett? "Their record may not be great but they have [Mashrafe] Mortaza, Shahadat [Hossain] and Abdur Razzak and it is a nice bowling line-up in their own conditions". He means 'nice' in the 'what does she look like, she is a very nice person' sort of way.

"They are going to be a formidable opposition for us". Have checked the thesaurus and formidable can also mean horrible. "We expect to win the series but we also know that it is going to be a tough challenge". A tough challenge, like opening the second pack of peanuts when your hands are slippery from the first pack.

"If we are not on top of our game then they can upset us. That's the thing we are trying to avoid here". The phrase 'top of our game' is interesting.

"Bangladesh know their conditions better than anyone and it is up to us to make sure that we are on the same level as them". They know their conditions better than anyone else, those cunning buggers.

Daniel, you enjoy your tour of wonderment, balloons, and magical gratification, while the rest of the team tours Bangladesh.

October 7 - Goodbye you giant alien lizard freak

Sourav Ganguly's touching retirement post. I have no time for Ganguly; I think he is over-rated as a cricketer, over-rated as a leader, and generally get in fights with his fans. By this time I was sick and tired of explaining why I didn't like him, so I just sent him on his way.

Sourav Ganguly has fucked off.

He is going to give it the goodbye tour and then we never have to watch him look nervous around short balls again. His kind has been sapping the lifeblood out of our kind since Jesus was a gleam in Moses' eye.

I know I should write some long and vitriolic piece about how Ganguly is an over-rated chunk of racoon sperm. But, who cares.

The Lizard is going. So some Indians will be happy. Some will be sad. And the rest of us really won't give a shit. That is a legacy.

Goodbye you Reptilian Martian, enjoy your stupidly named IPL team, and let the men play the real stuff.

October 10 - Kent, you're a bunch of arseholes

The word Kolpak is used in this post a couple of times. It was a word that sounds made up, but it is in fact the name of a Slovak handball keeper who changed the rules of county cricket thanks to the European Union, it's really boring, but means players from certain countries are considered part of the European Union and can play as "English" players in English domestic.... Just look it up.

My lack of love for South Africa is well documented. And I feel sorry for Kent. They got the raw deal from the BCCi and CA over the champion's league. They fell apart in the Twenty20 final. They got relegated from Division One in bizarre circumstances. And I like Joe Denly.

But perhaps they deserve everything they get. They signed Ryan McLaren, a young South African who can play, on a Kolpak deal for three years. He does a lot of bowling and he does a bit of batting, and in county cricket he does them pretty well.

So South Africa, in need of players who are actually exciting, gave Ryan a call. And he says sure, I'll play for my country, just let me tear up that contract I signed that said I won't play for my country. But Kent said no.

The new division two team took advantage of a loophole in county cricket, and instead of doing the gentlemanly thing, and helping out a young cricketer, they are putting the squeeze on him.

Now Ryan is not blameless here. What sort of an idiot signs a contract that says he can't play for his country for three years? It's not like this is IPL money; sure he would be comfortable with Kent, but he will make a lot more money as an international cricketer, which he has the talent to become. Kent signed a 25-year-old; this isn't some crusty old man, and they must have known that with his performances for them he had a chance to play for his country. So why be arseholes about it?

According to Kent they have built the team around him. Not whiz kid Joe Denly, proper quick Robbie Joseph, captain pie eater Rob Key, or the MVP of county cricket Van Jaarsveld. If I was Ryan I would feign a back injury or insist on bowling left arm orthodox to piss them off, although I probably wouldn't sign anything that said I couldn't play for my country for three years.

Legally I am sure Kent is in the right to keep him, but morally, this is fucked up. People dream of playing for their country, not of honouring three-year deals for Kent. Maybe the kid made a mistake, but Kent needs to get over it, and let him play for his country.

October 14 - Kiwi, the meaning of which is grit and determination

New Zealand fulfill Daniel Vettori's talk, just to make me look like an idiot.

We all know how hard it is to come from behind and win. It takes fortitude, strength of character, a certain canny nature, and big 'clang clang' balls. New Zealand has all that in spades; bucketloads of the stuff. One down against the monster force of nature that is Bangladesh.

Once you wake up Crashraful, you are in for a world of pain. That is not even mentioning the Bangladeshi Jamie Siddons Siddique, or marauding Mashrafe Mortaza. They are a team chock full of weapons, and Daniel Vettori knew this going in (I wrote about Daniel Vettori being in a fantastical wonderland if he believed Bangladesh were a real threat).

He was on the ball, his mind on the job, and taking it one match at a time, while the rest of you were taking the piss. Unfortunately the full force of Bangladesh cricket hit him square between the eyes like a mini hurricane of brass knuckles.

By the time he had left the bloody canvas New Zealand were one-zip down. But it takes a big knockout blow to take Daniel Vettori's merry men down. And somehow, with the grace of the aliens, Daniel not only broke even with them, but pushed ahead for a victory.

The joy. The jubilation. The sweet taste of victory against an opposition of the ultimate class when your back is not to the wall, but through the wall and down the street cowering in a corner.

New Zealand, we applaud you.

October 19 - Fairytales don't happen

Bryce is sent home from India.

The world is a horrible horrible place.

You will die. Your family will die. Your friends will die. Your turtle will die. That is life.

Death is inevitable.

Do you know what isn't inevitable? Shoulder injuries. Shoulder injuries that shatter the hopes and dreams of a young blogger and an old leggie.

Shoulder injuries that injure earthbound angels. Shoulder injuries that pull at the very fabric of love. Shoulder injuries that tear off your shirt and shit on your chest while you are waiting for the bus. Those kind of shoulder injuries.

When Bryce, the Facebook kid, injured his shoulder during the A tour, I was upset. When Bryce, Nice Bryce, was sent home with his shoulder injury from the Test squad, I was very upset. When Bryce, Cricket With Balls' Own, needs a shoulder injury that will have him out of action for the entire summer season, I was fucken crestfallen.

I have waxed lyrical about this before, but this time it is different. I am spent. There is nothing left. My Bryce well is dry. So please, a minute's silence for Bryce's Test career.

Surely not even he could provide a fairytale from here.

October 21 - Ricky gets a bit spanky

Australia start to unravel.

Brett Lee is in shit form. Only for the last two Tests. In this Twenty20 world though, anything that happened more than 12 days ago is hard to remember. Australia went to India with four bowlers. Lee, the best quickie in the world. Clark, the proctologist with the Just For Men rinse in his hair. Johnson, with the form in India, against India, and a tongue ring. And McGain, the only Test class spinner in Australia.

By the first Test McGain's shoulder was being prepped for surgery. For the second Test Clark's elbow was stuck in a bucket of ice. The best quick bowler in the world was expected to stand up. He didn't.

Maybe this is a hangover from his separation, maybe he's just not suited to India, or maybe he saw Hotel Rwanda on the way over and he hasn't got over his 'white guilt' just yet. We won't know. What we do know is that Ricky Ponting doesn't care. Couldn't give a shit. Doesn't give a fuck. Not one little cracker.

Ponting is not a reason sort of bloke, he is a results sort of guy. Lee isn't giving them to him, so he publicly shits in Lee's cereal. Whether this improves Lee's output won't be known until the next Test. We do know it didn't work with Dizzy Gillespie or Shaun Tait.

I don't have a problem with a bit of public flogging, but why are there different rules for batsmen than bowlers? Lee gets embarrassed in front of the world.

Can you name a batsman that Ponting has publicly embarrassed anything like this? Has Hayden ever been dropped down the order when he is struggling? When Katich couldn't hit the ball in 2005, was the batting order changed and Kasprowicz sent in before him? Has Michael Clarke's form ever been questioned when Australia is less than three for 150?

No.

The bowlers get spanked around by Ricky every time Australia is losing. If you want to be an arsehole Ricky, that is fine, but be an equal opportunity arsehole.

October 22 - The ten reasons why India beat Australia

Australia lost the second test to India, no excuses for the Aussies, well not from me.

They played better cricket
Dannii Minogue's nostrils
They played better cricket
El Nino
They played better cricket
They played better cricket
The credit crunch
They played better cricket

Symonds likes fishing
They played better cricket

October 22 - Dear Anil,

Australia seem to do ok against India when Anil captains, but when Dhoni does, not so much.

I need you. Things feel different without you. I am having trouble sleeping at night, food doesn't taste the same, and some of my arm hair is falling out from the stress. Back when we were together things were easier, everything was so perfect, we just clicked and you don't just give up on that magic.

You are hurting now, and I understand, but I need you to fight, for us. I know it was too high profile for you, and the papers printed all sorts of nonsense, but we have an electric connection, you cannot deny that. Sure we had our bad moments, but Sydney was a long time ago, and I made up for it in Perth, didn't I?

It's hard to find a good man Anil, and you are courageous, dignified, hot in a Ravi Shastri yet nerdy kind of way, and it's you I want to toss with. This new guy isn't the same. He isn't as polite, his hair has obviously been styled, and between you and me, I am not sure he is even 'one of us'.

You can't replicate what we had with someone else, remember it took two men to replace you. They say you're old, I say you're sophisticated. They say you're boring, I say you're dependable. They say you're past it, I say you're it.

You are the sunshine that warms up all my darker press conferences. You are the song I sing when I see a bird or smell a flower. You are the life force I need to make it though the hellish winter season. You are my everything. You do not merely complete me, you are me, and I you. We are the ying and yang of the cricket world, and when we are together there is nothing we can't achieve.

I wanna see you plough through the crease, over after over. I wanna see you let the ball come out the back of your hand. I wanna see that forehead drip with sweat, just for me.

I miss the way your hand feels before the toss. Come back my brown sugar lover.

I need you.

With hugs and kisses,

Your hairy little goblin Ricky

November 1 - The CWB Stanford Drinking game*

It was hard to get through the Stanford super series game without drinking.

Following on the great response to Miriam's drinking game for the IPL final, I have tried to follow in her footsteps. Use this wisely my friends, and if you can't drink responsibly, drink rambunctiously.

1 finger

A dropped catch (although two fingers if you think your mum could have caught it). Any standard Stanford sighting. A mention of the facilities. Discussions of Gayle's omission. Tony Cozier telling you about an Old West Indian Cricketer or adminstracrat. Mentions of the black bats.

2 fingers

A shot of Curtly Ambrose's mohawk. Bumble using the word 'pressure', or any word that is similar. Every time KP looks befuddled. Interview with a player on field who can't hear the questions, or any technical problems with interviews at all.

3 fingers

Any shots of the pool.

James Anderson sightings (down your glass if he looks moody). For overs where more than ten runs are scored. An example of green-eyed jealousy by a former player over the cash. If an umpiring decision is not referred and you think it should be.

Down your glasses

Anytime Stanford touches someone (handshakes excepted). When Emily Prior is shown. If the Stanford Superstars are called the West Indies.

Down your glasses with a drink you have bought on holidays.

If either team scores over 170.

Merry Drinking everyone.

*Not for use by the weak or the wounded.

November 2 - A tale of two series

Australia has played two Test series in one. The first one has been against Anil Kumble's team, and Australia has done pretty well against them, but can't take 20 wickets. The second series is against MS Dhoni's men, and in the first Test they were destroyed. Annihilated. Seriously fucked up.

So now that the king of the straight one is gone, Australia has a hell of a time levelling this series. Not only do they need to overcome their 20 wicket hoodoo, but they need to overcome Dhoni's magical waddle, and perhaps that is a bridge too far.

The Indian team love his swaying hips and can't wait to get into action with him. This should be enough to win the series even if Australia has regained some composure. So far this is not an exciting series; the best we can hope for in this Test is for both teams to have a chance of winning and no draws in sight on the fifth day.

November 3 - England think too much

The West Indian Stanford Super Stars XI beat England and collect 20 million dollars.

The Superstars won the money. They wanted to win, they thought about winning, they prepared to win. And they won.

Some would say that is how you play sport. England decided on a different tack. The selection process was not for a Twenty20 game, it was the One Day squad. Some new players were made to feel uncomfortable at their selection, like they had anything to do with it.

From there some players were talking about money, some were talking about India, some were talking about playing for their country. England arrived days before their first game. They all tried to sound unconcerned about money, even though the game was money. Then the wags and Stanford visits got to them. Then they lost the game. Peter Moores and KP believe their heads were not in the game.

But whose fault was that?

With Moores talking shit about what the game was about, and KP telling everyone to respect the crunch of credit, they had their boys all fucked up in the noggin. They were playing a team who wanted to win; for them it was the about the money and they have it.

Apparently KP told Gayle that that the Superstars needed the money more than his boys did. Perhaps he is a philanthropist after all. At least he didn't try to make the Windies grovel for their money. He just sort of gave it to them.

If that was the plan, they did it beautifully.

November 4 - Goodbye Anil

Anil finally retires.

No more straight ones, no more forehead wiping, and no more Anil.

The man is gone.

There will never be another Kumble. It is not possible. Being a leg spinner is hard enough, but to play at his level for this long without a ripping leg break is super human. It's like a porn star having a small dick. Or a porn star having no breasts. It just doesn't happen.

Somehow Anil made it work. That takes a special man, a great man. To rise above all the crap that goes on in Indian cricket and be a genuine match winner for over 100 Tests is amazing. He was written off so many times, but something in him just rose above it all. And that is why he is a champion.

He wasn't exciting, not even to a leg spinner, but he still won matches and contributed to his country winning games, and not many players can say they did that. Compared with the other great test spinners of his generation, he looks average. Like a boxer without a knockout punch, he is overlooked and underrated.

Sure Murali and Warne had the weapons, but Kumble could punch all day, or for all five days. He was never going to win as many fights as the other two, but he never stopped punching. I would say in the history of Test cricket there have been hundreds of bowlers more talented than Kumble. Yet he has out-lived, out-bowled, and out-muscled almost all of them.

That is a special player.

That is Anil Kumble.

Test cricket was lucky to have him.

November 5 - A modern love story about sledging

Gautam Gambhir was given a suspension for elbowing Shane Watson, not a medal.

I love sledging. It is great. Test cricket would be poorer if it were not there. Soft players like Graeme Hick might have had careers. Yuck.

So when Albie "I don't need to hear from Gautam" Sachs comes in and says it is against the spirit of the game, he goes straight into my Peter Roebuck file. Spirit of the game, spirit of my arsehole. I am so sick of this bullshit.

Sledging has always happened. Back in the day it was more gentlemanly by-play, and it included things like "here is my bunny and I'll bet you a thruppunenny you can't hit my wicket ol' chap". Times have changed, and so has the language.

Sledging has limits: racism is out, and homophobia will be next. No one likes to see a batsman be sent off. Other people probably have limits that I don't care about.

Gautam City Gambhir has made his name in this series. Before this he was a fringe Test batsman with a good white ball record. Everyone could see his talent, but he couldn't quite make it happen in Tests. He looked good early on against Australia, but they talked him out of his innings.

The minute he stopped scoring freely they were all over him, and he fell for it. Then he stood up, and he used the sledging to focus himself, and suddenly the boy who couldn't make a Test century become the man who made a double ton. Did he let it get to him, yes. Physically that manifested itself as an angry elbow.

But he used it to urge him on as well. Who knows if he would have had a series like this if the Australians hadn't forced him to concentrate. Now he leaves this series as a proper Test batsman. One who can take all the shit thrown at him, and make runs at the highest level.

'Tis a beautiful thing this sledging is.

November 7 - Australia's spin dilemma

Imagine you are held up in a castle, which is surrounded by zombies, and there are five people with you. One is a librarian, two of them are accountants, one is an unemployed X-Box champ and the last one a carpenter who did six months of kick-boxing. At this stage you are better equipped to survive the zombies than Australia is to find a spinner.

You think you know how bad Australia's spin options are? You really don't. Forget about White's straight 'uns, and Krejza's Krazy cameo on this Test. Back home the truth is even uglier. Three games into the domestic season and the number one spinning wicket taker is Marcus North with six wickets.

Marcus North is a batsman, a good one, and as a spinner is someone you bowl before a break, or when your state doesn't want to pick a real spinner. His career first class bowling average is 44.

Next on the list is Nathan Hauritz, occasional Australian tourist with a career first class bowling average of 49, and he has five wickets half way through his third game. How he still gets a first class game for NSWales is beyond me.

Behind him is Andrew Symonds, the best performing finger spinner Australia has had since Colin Funky Miller, but he is still in the doghouse over his fishing. Then Adam Voges, another batsman, who gets a bowl when Marcus North is tired.

Rounding out the top five is Aaron O'Brien of South Australia, who has a career first class bowling average of over 70, and a career batting average of 25. He proves if you can hold a bat you can get a game for South Australia at the moment. That is what Australia has to pick from.

They haven't had the best of luck with their spinners. Shane Warne retires to spend time with the ladies, Brad Hogg retires to tend to his sick lady, and Stuart MacGill retires because the fat lady was singing. Then they find Cricket With Balls' Own Nice Bryce McGain in an internet café searching dating sites, they offer him the job, he takes it, but his arm is stuffed from all those years of moving his mouse around and he can't bowl.

So what do they have left? A batsman who doesn't bowl himself in White, and an off spinner with a terrible record on the field and not much better off it in Krejza. Not to forget Beautiful Beau Casson who went from being a Test cricketer to not being a regular in his state side without playing a game in between.

Australia does not have a spin dilemma; they simply don't have spinners.

What they have is part timers (White, North, Symonds, and Voges) and journeymen (Krejza, Hauritz, Casson, and O'Brien).

There are young spinners coming through: Jon Holland from Victoria has impressed a lot of players in his first year, and Steve Smith from NSWales looks like a real talent. Unfortunately Dan Cullen, Xavier Doherty and Cullen Bailey have been "coming through" for so long now it looks like they have gotten lost.

If you were a selector looking for an Australian spinner right now, you'd probably prefer to take on a few zombies. You could argue that the selectors already have a zombie problem.

November 8 - Krejza, an Andalusian dog

Australia finally decide to unleash Jason Krejza for the fourth Test against India; a week earlier he was not ready for Test cricket according to Tim Neilsen and Ricky Ponting.

This never really happened, did it? Eight wickets, on debut, for a guy with a first class record that makes ordinary look great. It's a fucken surreal dream that should include ants coming out of hands.

We don't even know the dude though. Imagine you were Krejza's best friend, his lover, his mother. Hopefully not all three. But one of them.

And he was playing his first Test. What is the best result you could hope for? Perhaps Six wickets in the match; a handy two for in the first innings, and a plucky four wickets in the second. What would you be thinking as the wickets went down one by one.

Dravid, the wall, mounted by your little boy.
Sehwag, the God, struck down by your special guy.
VVS, the surgeon, sliced open by your main man.
Dhoni, the waddling model, sideswiped by your mate.
Ganguly, the Giant Alien Lizard, probed by the light of your life.
Then the tailenders, who are the cherry on top of your surreal little day.

Can you imagine how this would feel? Of course not, because we saw this shit, we don't know him, and half of us don't believe what we saw. Imagine what his family, friends and lovers must be feeling. Some of them must be thinking they just drank from one of Jason's spiked drinks.

They must be doubting their reality matrix at this stage. And if the freaky-deaky dream-like Krejza experience wasn't enough, then as they are coming down, a krab scuttles out and makes 90* off 120 balls.

Luis Buñuel couldn't make that shit up.

November 10 - And that's that

India defeat Australia at home, which is a familiar song, but this one sounds louder.

India win, India win.

They were the better team, and they closed it out quite well in the end. Australia were riding on the Christian Warrior's shoulders for a while. Then finally Amit Mishra was brought on.

He got one to fly into King Probot Hussey's gloves. Once Dravid completed the catch, which for him was quite an achievement today, Australia were finished. That was fitting, because in the only other Test where a side looked like taking 20 wickets, Mishra was the one who inspired India.

This was the best Test of the series, which wasn't hard; it was the only one where both sides could still win on the last day. India won, and even if they weren't so convincing at all times, they were by far the better side. Australia faced the media in a similar way to the way they played this whole series. They thought they were doing the right things, but instead they just kept making mistakes and baffling the rest of us.

The dark cloud of over rates hung over the day's play. India bowled four overs in the morning session, or so it seemed. Test cricket is now an after-lunch game, that is where all the overs are.

Things we learnt from today: Mishra handles pressure well, you can't keep standing on the leg side, and you can get a runner for being generally unwell. India now has to play against a team a little better suited to their conditions. Australia has to play the Bangladeshi slayers from New Zealand.

The more experienced team, which was were better suited to the conditions, and a better unit, won the day, the Test, and the series. India now needs to survive their transition period as the elderly gentlemen depart. Australia has shown the world that it is not that easy.

Neither team has long before their next challenges. Right now India will bathe in the glory of a two-zip win against the Aussies.

So they should.

November 11 - Could Dhoni be the best captain in world cricket?

It's a scary question, not because Dhoni can't captain, he can, but can anyone else? Australia has Ponting, who may not be in the job much longer.

Bangladesh has Crashraful, who while being the coolest batsman to watch go out, can't really find a way to teach the kittens anything, especially since he is still a kitten himself.

England have KP, who talks the talk and fires up his team mates, but so far seems to not really understand fielding positions or games for cash.

New Zealand plumped for Daniel Vettori, who has glasses, so people assume he is intelligent, but I haven't seen many occurrences of this just yet.

Pakistan doesn't have a team anymore, and when they did, they had a work experience kid looking after the boys.

Sri Lanka has Mahela, and lots of people rate him as a captain. I think he captains by numbers, and he never goes outside the lines.

South Africa chose Graeme Smith years ago, and just don't have the balls to get rid of him. He is improving as a captain; by the time he is 43, he will be a great one.

West Indies picked Gayle, who doesn't really want the job, but actually does a pretty good job from time to time in spite of it.

Not a golden era for captains. More a dark brown era.

Dhoni may not have been tested much so far (the Australian team certainly didn't provide much in his two Tests), but he has done well with limited opportunities. He won the Twenty20 smells-like-World-Cup thingy. He beat Australia and Sri Lanka during the Adam Gilchrist goodbye tour. He almost won the IPL, if it wasn't for the damn Warne. And he was two-zip in this series, while Kumble was zip-zip.

It's not so much the numbers though, it's the way he reads the game, the way he takes chances, and the way he builds up his team-mates. The worst captaining I have seen him do was on the fifth day, but that is the only time I have seen him be overly defensive and lose the plot for a little while.

We all saw the difference when Kumble left the field in the first Test; it was as if Dhoni went around taking out butt plugs from every player, or putting them in I suppose. The waddling model may turn out to be another dud, but right at the moment he is the closest thing world cricket has to real captain type captain, well, outside the IPL anyway.

Of course he would be a better captain if he regained his old hair cut.

November 11 - My dirty secret

No it's not rubbing myself in Vegemite while watching my DVD of "Where the Heart Is". That's not a secret. My secret is uglier and dirtier than that. It would mean that I would not be allowed in the Oval. It could end my career before it has started. It will make Lalit Modi hate me, way more than just reading my blog.

I have been watching the ICL.

It comes for free on the Zee Music channel in England; obviously I would not pay for it. But for free, I will rub it all over my body. Like the IPL, it's a culture shock watching it. Although the major culture shock is listening to Dean Jones commentate. He is like a bag full of coked up puppies at feeding time. When is isn't jumping around and screaming best catch/throw/shot/ball ever, he says things like "we have a saying back home, 'just have a fair dinkum go ya mug'", well we also have another saying back home: "fuck Dean Jones is a wanker".

Getting past him, they do have two people I like (obviously none of them are Tony Greig): a chick who does the interviewing, who is freakishly attractive, and Atul someone, an ex-Indian cricketer with a moustache that should be kept in a museum.

The level of cricket seems to be about English domestic level, but the waistlines are more village cricket-like. You can't watch more than a game every three or four days, and obviously if there is real cricket on, or repeats of Mash, there is no need to watch it.

The best bit about it is you get to see your favourite journeymen in full glory. My whole life I have wanted to see Jimmy Maher with a spare tyre under his top, and now I can. For me it is a nostalgic series, as a lot of my favourite cricketers never really made it at international level. Ian Harvey and Matthew Elliott were my two favourite players when I was younger, so to have them back is great. Elliott played a pull shot so nice the other day I could have poked the eye out of a cyclops with my erection. I miss that. Also over there is Ryan Campbell, who if he was Victorian would have been my favourite cricketer of all time. It's sort of like a Bollywood senior's tour.

There are also really camp uniforms, cheerleaders hidden from half the crowd, over-the-top commentating, a stupid phrase they say when people hit a six, and a bunch of Indian players most of us have never heard of.

No Bollywood stars though; instead the camera often pans to Daryl Cullinan, which is different. Everyone should watch one game, but perhaps only one. There is one serious problem with the league though; nothing to do with the cricket, or anything like that. The annoying logo in the corner that flashes and changes and looks like a 1980s music video effect. It's like having Tony Greig dancing Flashdance in the corner of the screen at all times.

November 12 - Pakistan vs the Lahore badass motherfuckers

Being that I have now admitted to watching the ICL, I can now tell you something wonderful that isn't just about chubby journeymen dominating Indian fringe players.

Lahore.

They are the Pakistani side in the competition. Watching them is like the first time you see a celebrity sex tape. They make other Twenty20 teams look like Novocaine addicts. They open up with a couple of Imrans, Farhat and Nazir. Nazir is one of those batsmen that hits the ball so sweetly you forget about life and taxes. He is a free spirit who deals in sixes.

Farhat is the more sensible one, but that's ok, cause in at three is Naved-ul-Hasan. He is sent in as a pinch hitter. There is nothing like a Pakistani pinch hitter; remember when Imran Khan used to come in and pinch hit, and occasionally come in and pinch block? Hasan just hits, and boy does he hit. You have to wonder why Pakistan never used his batting more often.

So once the dashers and sloggers are out of the way, the class comes in, starting with Mohammad Yousuf, not long ago one of the best three batsmen on the planet and still close to it. Straight after that is the man himself, Inzy, who smashed the ball around in the semi final like he would have in his prime. He runs the show, with Moin Khan, and he is just as cool as they have always been. Then to round out the top order is Azhar Mahmood, still one of the better slogging all rounders in the word, even if he has been in a good paddock or two.

The bowlers aren't shabby either. Mohammad Sami takes the new ball, and is still quick and silky smooth. Hasan and Azhar obviously get a bowl and then the ball is thrown to the greatest English Pakistani off spinner of all time, Saqlain Mushtaq. Fresh from being bored to death at Surrey, Saqi looks fresh and vibrant, and what's that Saqi, you have another ball to go with your teesra and your doosra (that you invented and Tony Greig claims he named)? I don't know what it is called, but it is like a leg cutter that slides on but looks like an off spinner. In the sheds is the genius of Grand Master Mushtaq Ahmed, and all they need to do is get his knee right for four overs at a time.

That is a cool as fuck line up. They stick out like dogs' balls on a mouse in this league: they have more class, more excitement and are more watchable than any other team.

But what about the real Pakistan? Lead by the work experience kid Shoaib Malik.

They do have exciting players: Misbah Ul Haq, also known as Misbah Cricket (©kingcricket.co.uk), Shahid Afridi is still there, Shoaib Ahktar is back, and Younis Elvis Khan. Salman Butt has a great name. Sohail Tanvir is the second best Twenty20 bowler in the world and the best bowler off the wrong foot. But I can't remember the last time I was excited to see Pakistan play.

They don't even have a spinner who invents new deliveries. Right now Lahore are everything Pakistan used to be.

Wildly unpredictable, compulsive viewing, dynamic, sexy, Inzy and better than a Kate Winslet and Natalie Portman session.

It's a shame we can't have it in the main team, but at least we have it somewhere.

November 12 – International Jihad on Slow Over Rates (or IJSOR for short)

You are the cricket public. You are the reason the game gets money, you are the reason the game is on TV, you are the reason players drive nice cars.

You are the game.

Don't even doubt that. This game is each and every one of us. So why do we get bent over? Why are you constantly short-changed? Why, day after day, do international teams not complete their overs?

Four West Indian quicks used to be able to do it (before they decided to ignore it). But teams with spinners can't do it. This is horse shit. It's not good enough. These captains, and their captaincy by numbers, should be able to get through at least, at the very least, 90 overs in the day, regardless of how many wickets are taken. They shouldn't need an extra half an hour, and there should be no excuses.

Slow over rates are a blight on our cricket. We want to see cricket, not captains running up to chat to bowlers four times an over. This must stop; we the international cricket fan community deserve better. Let us strike down the evil-doers, and show the powers that be that we care, and this disgrace shall stop right now.

Join in our Jihad, your game needs it.

This is a joint production with Sportsfreak.co.nz.

November 14 - Understanding Yuvraj

England arrive in India, and Yuvraj gives them a huge welcome for the One Dayers with back to back hundreds.

Don't bother. There is something odd in his wiring. His parents don't seem to be the most stable human beings, and this may have rubbed off on him. In 2003 at the World Cup I thought I had seen the coming of a legend. In 2008 he still hasn't come. That's one horrible case of blue balls.

I wouldn't have believed in '03 that by '08 he wouldn't have been a Test fixture, but Yuvraj is an enigma wrapped in a pair off designer sun glasses. On a day like today he can do anything; it is like he is carrying a wand. His timing is supernatural, and few before him make it look easier. Then on other days I have seen more life from a blow up doll. He gets in the way of the ball and his bat, and he buys time until he is dismissed.

Today he brutalised England, Straw Dogs-like. In three months time, though, he will look like a hatched chick out on the crease. After his greatest achievements, he quite often puts in his weakest ones. In Australia he was pitiful, yet right before that he smote the Pakistanis all around. He doesn't make sense. Of course, he doesn't have to.

He can be an enigma, have a good career, make lots of money, and get lots of women. Maybe that's all he wants, and if so good on him; we will take what we can get.

Somewhere inside him there must be a fire to be more than a cameo man. To be the legend his talent would deserve. If for nothing else than to compete with Dhoni.

For the ladies. Of course.

November 15 - If I were Shivnarine Chanderpaul

The West Indies play Pakistan (some countries still do), in One Dayers in the Emirates, and Shiv carries them, again.

Firstly I would take that stupid black tape off my face. Then I would retire from international cricket. I figure I have, like, five years of county cricket left in me, two or three of IPL, maybe two or three of ICL after that.

But I can't do it if my back is broken, and I have been carrying this fucking useless excuse for a team for so long now I can hardly fucken walk. Every fucken time I walk out in the maroons, or my whites with my maroon hat, I have to pick up ten men, and carry them around for a day, and sometimes five. This really ruins the vertebrae.

Today was the perfect situation. We bowled Pakistan out for 230. I should have had a small role to play, maybe a 30 odd at the end, just a nice little average pumper. Instead I end up making more than half the runs. Sure I really boosted the average, but I am sick of this.

I want to play in a team. When I played for Durham this year, they had other batsmen, and we won. I liked that. I would like to do that again, but when I wear maroons it doesn't happen. Instead I have to do everything.

I get to the ground early, I cut the oranges, I roll the joints, I go back to the hotel, make the day's lunches, I drive the players' bus (bloody Dhoni stole that from me) back to the ground, I sit on Stanford's lap, I rub sunscreen on Brendan Nash's pasty white arse, and it's still not enough.

So this is my retirement. You useless fuckers can go on without me. If you get a real team, call me; I'll be playing with a winning team in Durham or a real Test team in Bangalore.

Thanks for the millions.

November 16 - Nazir's anti-nadir

It's hard to get too excited over a dashing ton in Twenty20 cricket. There may be a lot of sixes and fours, but the batsman gets a license to swing away. The game is designed for sixes, so when they happen they don't have the same impact on you as a Test six would. It's part of the reason why traditional cricket lovers aren't fawning all over the game.

Today Imran Nazir shit all over that theory. He hit 11 sixes in 44 balls on his way to 111* to win the ICL final for the Lahore Badass Motherfuckers. Like Chris Gayle and Prince Brendon before him, he was so dynamic that even though the game was designed for him to do what he did, you didn't care.

A six off the first ball over extra cover makes you forget about formats and average attacks and makes you sit back and gawk in geekish wonderment. Had this been the first time you had seen Imran Nazir bat you would have been excused for thinking he was the best batsman of all time. Had you seen him before you would have been excused for asking for a piss test.

I can't really explain the innings for you. You either saw it live, or you will never truly understand it. You can get too carried away with the ICL form, like the commentators do, but the truth is hitting doesn't get much cleaner than that.

And he was injured. This week has been a good time to be an injured batsman. Yuvraj was injured while he was smashing England for hundreds, and two of his drives were just amazing viewing, sixes off yorkers straight down the ground; he just played himself in and then let go.

Nazir just exploded from ball one. Few batsmen can do that, and even fewer of them can do it like this. The game was over at that point. It was brutalism personified. As a spectacle it would have been worth the admission several times over. As a great knock, well it was in a second rate domestic tournament, but you can only beat the bowlers you face.

November 17 - Prior & Bell: a product review

Roy & HG are sport-based comedians, but they are actually funny and knowledgeable, and would become famous in 2009 when Andrew Symonds labelled Brendon McCullum a lump of shit on their show. England's tour of India was still in One Day mode, and Yuvraj wasn't their only worry.

The great Roy & HG often referred to opening partnerships like law firms. Their most famous one was Mott & Elliott, which before Matthew Mott started getting courted by the Kiwis was the only time he had ever been mentioned outside a scorecard.

Now we have Prior & Bell, the phone company. Unfortunately this is not a company you want for your country. The wiring is all wrong.

Let's start with Bell. Like the late great Shane Watson, he is technically almost perfect. The problem with the perfect system comes when it needs to be flexible and adaptable. It cannot, and it is so fixed into the correct position that no different position can be formed. The owners of the technique know it cannot be adapted, but believe its absolute class will win the day; so far that has failed, and now people are even doubting this system ever had absolute class.

Prior is being sold as a dynamic new player on the mobile front. The record does not suggest that; his connection rate is infrequent, and when he does connect quickly, it drops out soon after. The marketing men have done a good job of the selling, but the customer feedback is horrible. There is a chance that this product is just being aimed at the wrong market. If it were rebranded, and moved into a niche, it may survive, but it does not have the reliability or true dynamics to be a mobile carrier at the top of the market.

When you combine the two, you end up with a service that simply does not work. They do not cover each other's shortfall, and, combined, make a terrible communications bundle. Instead of highlighting each other's strengths, they exacerbate the problem of the other system. We are not saying they would not work well separately, we just think that you deserve better for your cash. Why pay for fibre optics cables and take two tin cans and a ratty piece of string?

It's the users who get the raw end. The big company has so many failures in this market, that they are afraid to ditch these new products, even though these are clearly more failures. Interestingly there is another product the company are working on that people are very excited about; it's still experimental, but the new internet system, Steven Davies (in beta mode), has the techies purring.

November 18 - Ricky's cocoon of self denial

This was in response to Ricky Ponting putting his place in the following Test above winning a Test for Australia (which would have levelled the Indian series) by bowling part timers to catch up with the slow over rate instead of pushing for victory, and then getting pissed off with ex-captains for questioning him.

Ricky is angry with the very men that have made him possible. He is a grumpy never-likes-to-lose captain. Where do you think he got that from? Run a line from Steve Waugh to Allan Border to Ian Chappell and there you have it. Ricky doesn't see why they bagged him. He is deep in the Australian cricket team cocoon. The one that thinks dropping Symonds was the right thing to do, and the one that thinks that had Krejza played one week earlier he would not have been ready.

The truth is Ricky, no matter how much you and Tim tell us you did the right thing, we aren't buying it. As an Aussie Rules football fan you should know why. How many footballers have been rubbed out in the grand final to win it, and not given a flying fuck about the first game next season.

Apparently Symonds has admitted to his wrongs, and that is a good thing. Then why can't Ponting admit he made a mistake here? And while we are at it, why can't the whole selection committee admit they should have picked Krejza a week earlier?

There is no point being angry at Border or Chappell; they both would have set themselves on fire to win a game for Australia. You didn't, and that is why they bagged you, so stopbeing such a stroppy little prick and admit you made a mistake. It's not that hard, we have all made them Ricky; I once wore happy pants.

November 20 - Braddin your time is now

I knew Brad Haddin would get the number one keeping job. I wouldn't have picked him, but the selectors now love picking well performed 30-year-olds, and Haddin had been the apprentice for so long, Ronchi never stood a real chance. If that is how they are doing it, so be it, but eight Tests in and where are the performances?

His keeping has been average at best (he has played injured instead of letting replacements in), his batting, while being handy, has not been near his Shield standard, and so far he has not provided any impact. Going out to a Jesse Ryder straight one, with a loose shot on the up.

He is lucky though, because Luke Ronchi has not been firing for the Warriors this year. If he was, Haddin might be told he has the summer to settle the spot. The only keeper in Australia to be batting at an average over 30 is Tim Paine. And this is his first full year of wicket keeping at Shield level.

The boy is a freak, no doubt, but he has never had a full break out year with the bat, and it took him forever to get rid of Clingleffer for the main spot with the gloves. All this is helping Haddin, but the selectors won't keep him around forever. In India he was batted ahead of Cameron White, so the selectors still believe in him, but for how long? He is older than Ronchi and Paine, and the one thing we know about Ronchi is impact.

The boy is all impact, and when Haddin let him come in for the One Dayers in the West Indies Ronchi made 60-odd off 30-odd. People tend to remember that. Now Haddin is at home, on the pitches that suit him, he has to perform.

All we want is for him to bat like he does for NSWales, just back himself and play aggressively. Too many times he has gone into some sort of foetal position; just bat like yourself. Brad.

Australia is not good enough to carry someone anymore.

November 20 - In bed with **MS Dhoni**

This is adults only, as children should be shielded from sex at all costs, because it is not a natural part of life.

You hear about him before you see him; he doesn't have much of a reputation, but there is a buzz about him. Then after a drunken night you find yourself in a closet with him, and while he doesn't move the way you would like, he gets the job done.

The quickies are fun with him, and you decide he could be a keeper. So you set about planning a long-term relationship with him, but he doesn't perform for you at all, and at times he has trouble even getting erect. You figure the long-term serious stuff is not his thing, so you break it off.

Occasionally you text a young guy, and there is still the odd rendezvous with your favourite classy old man. But there is something about MS (maybe it's the hair), and you can't discard him so easily. You have fun with him, and more than often he gets you off, and you can't really argue with that. He keeps calling and calling, and eventually you fall for him again; this time it's on his terms, and then you're in an ongoing casual thing with him. With him in charge it all goes great, but you still think you may want more, but he has nothing of it, and even though not everything runs smoothly, you trust his judgment.

Then your relationship goes back to the quickie mode. Usually you'd be disappointed with the frivolous nature, but you are besotted with him now. Usually you'd need two other beaus at once to feel this excited, but you haven't returned the calls of Partiv in ages, and Anil can no longer get you there.

You have decided Dhoni is going to be your guy, but the constant speed gets to him, and he needs a break. It cuts you deep, and you doubt whether he is going to be there in the long run. You continue seeing the older gentleman and even the younger guy, even though you know it isn't the same.

Dhoni gets jealous by this and comes back out of the woodwork. Now he seems fit and hungry, and he is even willing to do things with you that you cannot believe. At first these strange erotic things worry you, but in his soft hands you feel secure. However now he seems calmer and more mature (might be the new hair), and you let him be in charge any way he wants to.

When you first feel that silk scarf around your neck, ever tightening, you start to panic, but he puts you at ease, and by the end, you and he fall deeper in love. You know he is the man for you, and your heart skips a beat every time he waddles in your direction.

November 21 - Michael Slater, a fan of the Balls

"He's got an unusual style Simon Katich. He's a, his nickname is… Well as a batsman could be crab if you like. Given he has a crab-like move across his stumps."

That was Michael Slater on Channel 9's coverage of the cricket. It went live to air, and literally dozens of people heard it. Now I am not saying I invented the phrase, people have used crab for years, but a quick look on Google suggests I have been at the head of the queue to popularise it, and I was definitely the first person to call Katich the Krab.

Now, with that in mind, and the fact Slater went to say "His nickname is the crab", I put it to you dear jury, was he in fact just regurgitating this site? Is Michael Slater a fan of the Balls?

Stranger things have happened. Do he and Bill sit at the back of the commentary box sniggering at sex posts about MS Dhoni? Why not.

Is this time for me to stop with the poor taste Michael Slater jokes? Of course not.

November 23 - Dear Simon,

We've had our up and downs. Ok, mostly downs. There has always been a certain friction between us. I blame you; that technique is grating on the eyes, and of course there was the leaving a neutral state for the devil so that you could get a Test cap. People could say I was overly harsh at times; sure they remembered the '05 ashes and some of them even remember you opening with Gilchrist, but they thought that with 'another' extended run you could come good, and no one deserves as much vitriol as I gave you.

They were wrong. They never saw you in state cricket, shuffling around like a demented hermit krab scoring at a strike rate that could bore Boycott. They don't know the pain you have put me through. Watching you bat was like getting an enema from a bear with chainsaws for hands.

I still feel that way.

But, just because aesthetically you pain me, does not mean I cannot see your niche in the team at this very moment. You are the coal miner in a bunch of stockbrokers and accountants. I am not just saying that because you are dirty a lot of the time, and because I cough when I think of you. Right at the moment the Australian team needs someone to make ugly runs.

Sure that hurts me to say it, but it's true. Almost every other time you have played, this has not been the case. Obviously a lot of those times were the selectors' fault, but with you krabbing around I took it out on you. Occasionally I may have gone too far. Probably not though.

Anyway, your four hundreds in eight Tests have placated my anger. Don't think I have gone soft though Mr Katich; if you fuck up I will fling enough faeces and bile at you to drown an elephant. Right at the moment you are doing ok, so don't fuck that up, and I'll try to keep the insults down to the bare minimum of one per post.

Cheers
Jrod

PS I'm still going to call you the Krab, especially now it is Michael Slater approved.

November 24 - Symonds fishes for trouble

Andrew Symonds was out drinking with rugby players and got a bit shirty with a autograph hunter, one Test after his re-inclusion in the Australian Test team that had just beaten New Zealand at the Gabba.

Symonds is back. Not in form. But in trouble. This time it is being involved in a bar altercation. Unfortunately it all sounds pretty tame, and he didn't hit anyone with a barramundi. Shame. Apparently some dude had a go at him in a pub that James Sutherland would never drink in. Luckily for you I have an updated copy of the players' conduct conditions that all Australian cricketers must sign.

Symonds has broken several clauses:

17.67a Drinking alcohol is fine, but you cannot drink in any bar that thinks Bundy and Coke is a cocktail.
88.96c Players may stay out 'til dark, but must be tucked up in their hotel room bed by the time the first episode of CSI or Law & Order is being shown in Australia.

1a Thou shall never drink with rugby players. If you have to slum it, find an Aussie Rules player.
65.23d Australian cricketers will have no personality.

This means the end for Symonds. Under these rules he will be put down at a simple ceremony out the back of Radelaide oval, just near the place where Mark Cosgrove hides his pizza boxes.

November 25 - A cricketer speaks his mind: he thinks about sushi

Anyone who has ever read a ghosted article by a cricketer, or a 'blog' written by a cricketer, will know of the excruciating pain. It's like being sent to a concentration camp, or listening to Wham. But Iain O'Brien has smashed all previous expectations of cricketers typing.

How? On a blog, his own blog. A cricketer with a regular non-paid Blogspot blog. He reports from each Test day. So far that is only at the Gabba, and some thoughts from the tour game.

I love it. These are some of my favourite moments from the aptly titled iainobrien.blogspot.com. "Lunch was sushi", "Back to the hotel and I get a phone call from the NZ Cricket president, not the normal call. He was bringing over the first 'prototype' of my underwear." "Finger up, I'm off! Arse! Really not the day I was hoping for!", "I don't know how many times I've been called a 'fagot' this afternoon!" "I really hate loosing", "I asked for the bowling machine to be 'cranked' up, in order to try to get used to the pace that will be coming at me in the middle. Shit it was quick", "My left tit to be precise. That hurt, and not how I wanted to play it", "NZ vs Aust - Gabba - Day Three ... and we're in the shit."

If cricketers said to the press, we're in the shit, more often, the world would be a better place. So get over to read a bit of Iain, 'cause fuck knows NZC will try and shut it down as soon as they can. I am sure it breaks some sort of rules that some sort of suit has drawn up.

November 26 – Hauritz to hell

I don't know how it happened. I don't know why it happened. And I don't care. Just fucken fix it. Get Hauritz out of Radelaide.

He can only do harm. Under no circumstances can he be Australia's spinner. Not on my watch. Dan Cullen, Aaron Heal, Jon Holland, or Xavier Doherty I would except. Not Nathan.

It is a pointless exercise. At least the others show potential. Nathan is gone, finished, he doesn't even get wickets at the SCG anymore. He was stamped, never again, years ago, and that stamp only comes off with brilliant Shield performances. Not mediocre drivel.

Six wickets at 50 in three matches does not a Test match earn. Sorry, I went Yoda there, but this is important.

This isn't India, so Australian spinners don't get a free Test here. Hauritz is just not up to it. He got out bowled by Michael Clarke in his only Test. His bowling average makes Krejza look like a superstar. He averages fewer than two wickets a game over 40 first class games. The majority of those were probably at the SCG, the spiniest pitch in Straya. Not once has he got a five-for.

And to top that off he is only 27. Ok that has nothing to do with it. But, he has had seven years to make a mark, and nothing. So many other spinners have made a mark since him. Cullen's record isn't that much better, he averages only eight runs less, but he has taken four five wicket hauls in five class cricket from only four more matches. He is bowling as averagely as Hauritz in Shield cricket this year, and this is his home pitch.

Or we could just not pick a spinner, since the only one performing in Australia is Marcus North.

November 27 - A catastrophe hits the world

After being mentioned in the media, and causing a furore with the faggot controversy at the Gabba, all Iain's blogs are to be vetted by NZC.

This is a sad day for cricket. People are in mourning. People are checking in with loved ones. The world seems a colder, darker place.

Iain O'Brien's blog is to be vetted by men in suits. I feel dirty just writing it. It was bound to happen. Perhaps I am to blame. Perhaps Uncle Rupert is.

Either way, we may never know if Iain finds the perfect pair of jeans now, as surely that will be vetted. This is a sad day.

November 27 – Everyone out

Day of the Mumbai terrorist attacks. England pull out of the rest of their One Day series, and the cricket world, and probably the real world too, is in shock.

Why does it take multiple people dying for a One Day series to be called off? Surely there could be a dead rubber/dull as shit clause in seven series One Dayers, to spare us from games that have no meaning. Or in the case of One Dayers, even less meaning than usual.

The terrorists probably didn't have this in mind. They probably just wanted to kill some people to prove some point. And before you go saying, well they are obviously cricket lovers, and couldn't bear to watch a seven-match series that was decided after four matches. Remember this, their actions have also cancelled the ICL and the Champion's League doodad.

How many friends will that buy them?

Terrorists, outside of Che and few others, have never been very good at PR. This is a sad day for all the victims, but this also affects world cricket. And let us not forget that if this happened in a non-cricket country, few of us would know about it.

So with cricket in mind, what does this do to world cricket? Whities are already afraid to go to Pakistan, add India to that, and world cricket is fucked. The fact that terrorists were looking for Whities will have the Whities' panties in a bunch for years to come.

With so few real Test nations, can we really afford to lose another one, especially the financial powerhouse? Few other sports can be damaged by terrorism more than cricket.

Will cricket survive it?

November 27 - Was Gavin Busy?

The tension is killing me. Is he in, is he out? What is Gavin Robertson doing these days? Will Nathan Hauritz get the luckiest Test cap since Shaun Young?

Why won't they name the team dagnabbit.

November 27 – Fuck

Hauritz is in.

November 30 - Has Dan fooled us?

We all assumed that Daniel Vettori was a smart man. He has glasses. His beard looks very maths professor-like. He is known as the thinking woman's crumpet. He looks like a famous literary character. Bowls spin. And generally makes sense when he talks.

This Test he has really tested that assumption. He is clearly injured, and fielding at mid off/on. You might say "so what?" Well have you ever been to the Radelaide oval? It's like a million metres long. In general you shouldn't put bowlers at mid on or off if they are required for big spells.

In this case it is even more stupid. He is injured, he is captain, and he bowled twice as many overs as any other player. That is dumb cricket. A day and a half of dumb cricket.

November 30 - Braddin rocks Radelaide

Against the Kiwis in Adelaide Brad Haddin finally makes some runs, and then some.

Brad Haddin just made the innings all his supporters have been waiting for. It was a top knock. Especially to see him brutalise the Kiwis.

Australia weren't in a lot of trouble before he made it, but they wouldn't have finished many in front of New Zealand without him. But let us not get the nipple clamps, battery objects or gimp masks just yet. This was on a flat batting pitch. Against the eighth ranked team in world cricket. With an attack not suited to the conditions. An injured strike spinner. And a simple chance being put down.

So it's good, and impressive, but it still needs to be seen in perspective. This was the breakthrough innings, but only last Test he dropped a catch he shouldn't have been going for. The good news about this innings is that he batted NSWales style. The Haddin before this was not the NSWales one, this one was. He took on the bowlers. He backed himself. And he changed the game.

Without him, New Zealand still had a hope. With him, New Zealand looked like a battered house wife/husband/same sex partner/blow up doll. If he keeps batting like this, he will make more than one eye catching Test century, and Luke Ronchi and Tim Paine will have to wait a lot longer.

Haddin's real test is against South Africa. What this has done is bought him lots of time. And if you are going to make a Test century, you might has well make one people will remember.

'Twas a rollicking good time innings, although maybe not so much for the Kiwis.

December 1 - Geoff is angry and he has a point, just not a correct one

Geoff Lawson, former ordinary coach of a bunch of teams, says England pulling themselves out of India smells of hypocrisy. That isn't true, it smells of poo-stained undergarments. Lawson believes it is a double standard that the Ashes went on in 2005 after the bombs on the trains, and they left this time. I have used a similar argument before, only for Australia, and I was right. Of course.

Australia wouldn't tour Pakistan, even though they were not the targets. England left India because people with guns were cutting down Whities (not in all occasions, but it only takes one to scare a Whitie). See the difference Geoff? It's tiny, but it's there.

Lawson is not way off the mark here, terrorism happens everywhere, and as far as I know the only terrorist action ever aimed at cricket directly was at the MCG, and I think it was for a footy game anyway. This was different to normal terrorist actions.

Bombs are indiscriminate. They are the lazy way, or the populist way, of getting rid of people. This was people going from hotel to hotel with guns looking for Whities, Poms and Yanks especially, to kill. The English cricket team stay in hotels. All cricket teams stay in hotels in India. Not all teams go to the ground on the Tube.

The chances of a player being caught in the Tube, mid-tour, during a terrorist attack are smaller than Natalie Portman doing a strip tease act with a cricket bat as a prop for my 30th birthday. Or at least the same. So that is the difference, which is why England went home instead of playing two useless One Dayers. That is why Harmy doesn't want to go back for the Tests.

The players are scared, because their nationality, at a hotel they stayed at, was targeted. Terrorism scares them, but indiscriminate bombs in public areas they can live with. They might not like them, but they can live with them, because they are not aimed at them.

This was aimed at them, and for someone like Harmy, who would have never left the north of England without cricket, that is scary. With all that in mind England are planning on coming back, "The ECB has informed the Indian Board it has agreed to tour India and play two Tests, the first at Chennai from December 11-15 and the second at Mohall from December 19-23. The tour will be officially cleared after discussions between the ECB's security consultant and officials in India, N Srinivasan, the BCCI secretary, said".

Maybe without Harmy, but he doesn't like travelling at the best of times.

December 10 - England goes all rainbow coalition and wristy on us

After a lot of back and forth England decide to go back to India for the Tests. Andrew Strauss and KP seem to have a lot to do with this decision.

Apparently there is still to be a Test series between England and India. Although nationality boundaries are so broad these days that this could end up being a tour of a combined professional cricketers XI vs India. England has Saffas, Indians, Pakistanis, Australians and Danes over there. Plus Graeme Swann, who is a spider from Mars. England have recently added to their squad, one officially, and one unofficially. The official one is Amjad Khan, who sounds like he should be slaying people in a David Lean film. He is a quick from Kent, and while not the quick from Kent I would pick (proud passionate paid-up supporter of Robbie Joseph), still a pretty decent quick bowler.

The unofficial squad member is Adil Rashid. Potential CWB cult figure. Part Pakistani, Part Yorkshirian, and all leggie. I am not sure what an unofficial squad member does, other than not pose for the group tour photo. What these two men do have in common is their brownness, and not from tanning, but from ancestry in the subbie. While South Africa masturbates all over the quota system, England just gets the job done. Shah, Monty, Bopara, Dimi and Patel have played in recent times.

Robbie Joseph can't be far away. And in county cricket there are other non-whites in the mix. It could be a racial extravaganza. An orgy of religions and skin tones. Like Woodstock, except not as well marketed.

Of course Khan and Rashid may still be a way off, and someone more cynical, like me, may even suggest that England has:

a) Run out of white players willing to go to the subbie
b) Run out of players they think can perform in the subbie
c) A variant of jungle fever, known as the curry cough
Or
d) Wanted the commentators to be able to say wristy more often

This is a good time to be brown in England. Look at Mushie: can barely speak English, has a multi-coloured beard, and follows a religion that makes most people think of exploding trains, and yet is gainfully employed on a part time basis by the ECB.

Is that not what we all want, brown middle aged men working part time for Giles Clarke? What a wonderful world it will be.

December 13 - Rahul, you've done enough

Rahul Dravid continues to define misery while he bats against England.

Please India, please put Dravid out of his misery. I can't do this any longer. I can't watch him at the crease. I can't stand him in this kind of pain.

If you have any heart at all, put him down. I am sure he can average 30 runs a year for the next two years on sheer grit and determination. But this is not the Dravid we fell in love with; he is a cadaver holding a bat. It saddens me that youngsters will remember Dravid as that dude who stood in front of the stumps for an hour or so at a time before departing them. There was a time when he was king. At that time his forward defence could give you an erection that could kill Jesus.

He was nicknamed The Wall for good reason: getting through to the stumps was like deflowering the girl who runs the born again Christian chat room. While his Indian peers batted with flamboyance and panache, he batted like a starving dude fighting for the last loaf of bread for his family. And a lot of us loved him for it.

Now he is holding on a little too tight. The magic has left him, he may still make the odd fighting half century, he may even arse a century, but this is not the man we loved. He is a photocopy of a replica that was taken from an out of focus picture in a dark and dreary rain storm.

Dravid, your fans will always love you, but stop torturing yourself, careers finish, but legends remain.

Leave now, because you are too good to be dropped.

December 14 - Shiv makes a hundred by proxy

The West Indies tour New Zealand to battle out who is really the best of the worst Test teams.

Jerome Taylor has a Test century. Weird. Jerome's top score before this was 31, perfect preparation for a Test century. 31 in 33 innings after 20 Tests, and then bang, a hundred.

At a run a ball as well. No fucking around there. But as usual, non-captain marvellous, aka lord mega chief of gold, aka Shivnarine Chanderpaul, saved the day, as he gave Taylor some advice. He said "bat and bat and bat".

What better advice could you give a man with no half century in first class cricket? That is the problem with most batsmen, they bat and bat and then go out. If they could just bat and bat, and bat, they would make more centuries.

That is the thing about Shiv; even when he doesn't make hundreds, he makes hundreds. How many other batsman can boast that? Not many.

This advice is gold though. Ask Jerome; he was asked to do it once, and he made a hundred. You should try it.

December 15 - From the pulpit

England dominate the first Test against India, they set a target of 387 and then Sehwag comes out...

It is beyond any comprehensive description. I didn't even see it live. Just after it finished I was watching the replay, and it left me dumbstruck and silent. Not particularly amazing on its own, but being that I was at a bar ordering a breakfast beer at the time, it lends a certain extra credit to it.

I was standing at the bar, money in hand, thirsty, but there was no ordering from me. Apparently the barman asked me for my order, three times. I was transfixed.

Our man was on the screen. He was murderous. I have never seen anything like it. I would give my exceptionally special little toe to a stranger for the chance to go back in time and see it live. He was pure adrenaline, he was dancing on sharks, he was killing Nazi shop-keepers, he was destroying every last thing in front of him.

Beer could not compete. Nothing could.

I almost punched the barman when he broke me from my happiness bubble. "Good God man, have you no sense of history, look at what this man, nay prophet, nay God, is doing", is what I would have said if words would have come to my lips. Words however were nowhere near my mouth. Wonderful magically amazingness was all around. He was not just batting, he was carving his name into the memory of every person lucky enough to see him.

You cannot forget what you saw. It was what eyes were invented for. Obviously.

When Harper finally ended the best short moment any of us are ever going to have, all we were left with was deep sorrow and terrible heartache. Because he is not a batsman, anyone can bat, he stands above all that, and what we get is light, and hope.

I even forgive him for making me forget about having a beer.

There should be no argument, you must Practise Sehwagology now.

December 15 - Strauss defeats the evil-doers

George W Bush wanted to destroy terrorism. He tried Dick Cheney, billions of dollars, bombs, war, and Christianity, all to no avail.

That is because he didn't use Andrew Strauss. Andrew Strauss is the ultimate weapon for taking down terrorism. While everyone else was scared of going back to India the man said that we owe it to cricket to come back, and he said it so well that even Harmy went back.

Then as the Indian crowd, Indian team, English team and everyone else wasn't sure what the correct response was, Strauss showed them. He stiff upper lipped a hundred. Then, to stick his bat handle long and hard up the anal passage of the terrorists, he makes another one.

It's like he said "take that, and that".

Strauss is the sort of guy you want protecting your daughter's virginity, as he takes the shit seriously. In fact I wouldn't play him unless it was to protect a woman's reputation, or if a madman was threatening the world with a nuclear bomb. That is when you get the best out of Strauss.

The man bats for a cause. The rest of the time is just filler.

England may have lost the Test, thanks to Sehwag's magic and Sachin's poise, but Strauss' two innings stands over it all.

December 16 - Monty does not have an adaptive mind

They aren't my words. I would have said he was a dumb fuck when bowling. But both sentiments are true. Monty just cannot think. He can spin the ball a lot, he can hit an ant's dick at 22 yards. And he goes all day long.

What he doesn't do is change with the situation. When his normal line and length fail him, there is no other plan. Even bowling machines can change line and length. Monty just falls apart. He has no creative bone in his body.

The Indians were brutal on him, and he just didn't seem to know where to go. People are already saying that if one spinner is required they would prefer the Swann from Mars. The selectors will pick two spinners, and even if they didn't, Swann would be dropped.

Monty's honeymoon ended a long time ago, and now it's his time to keep the vultures off his back. Or the Swanns.

See what I did there. Genius.

December 17 - Cricket with balls lament

South Africa tour Australia, the unofficial Test championship.

We should be excited. South Africa vs Australia is our favourite series. But, we miss him. Our heart is heavy. We almost feel lost without him. The poor fucker is sitting in the hills drinking absinthe out of a goat's liver, and we wish he was playing.

Andre Nel is more than a player.

He is a mental case performance artist with homicidal tendencies. They don't grow on trees. Not even in the tropics. This series doesn't have a lot of personality in it. Smith used to be entertaining when he was a cocky dickrod, but that has gone. Symonds was more fun when he was less grumpy. Who else?

Morne Morkel, at a stretch, might provide some light-hearted moments if he breaks down mid-over again. Truly entertaining figures seem thin on the ground.

Andre could make up for all of that, and then some. Unfortunately, we may never see the crazy fucker again. He will be sorely missed.

As will the goat.

December 17 - The Krab is #1, Australia's ugly truth

Australian cricket was changing fast, and two men that I had criticised were now holding up the side, and as much as I am an arsehole, I give credit where credit is due, mostly.

As much as I hate to say it, and I say it through a grinded arsehole, Simon Katich is Australia's best batsman right now. When the shit is hitting the fan, if he is not out, you can feel some sort of comfort. He is still ugly, oh how he is ugly, but he is a banker. With Hayden and Punter looking increasingly shaky, the Krab's hard exterior is getting the job done.

The South Africans were a cock in a hoop at 3/15, but intelligent Australian cricket fans, those who read my site, knew that the Krab would be hard to shift. He sort of digs into a crease. And when you try and get him out, he shuffles, he nudges, and from time to time, he swipes.

Bugger me if hours later he isn't always there. The old Krab, the early '00s edition, wouldn't swipe, didn't nudge enough, and was usually put out of his misery after hurting everyone's eyes. Now, with a technique just as fugly, he makes it work. It would hurt my head to work out how it works, but it does. He won NSWales a Shield title doing it, and now he is saving the bacon of men who get paid far more.

Damith (theflyslip.net) said this, "What fucking balls, ugly and untidy as fuck but gets the bloody runs on the board". That is exactly what he is doing.

My biggest problem with Katich is that when he played for Australia, there were no runs. In his first painful 23 Tests, he made two hundreds at 36. In his last 10 Tests, four hundreds at 61. No one has a better record in the Australian team this year. And no one looks worse doing it.

Keep up the hard work, Krab.

December 18 - Mitchell is a stud

Australia was living its nightmare, the sad reality that 20 wickets in a Test were going to be hard even at home. Between the flat pitch, and the two settled batsmen, Australia was going to have to get lucky. Australia didn't look like taking a wicket. If a wicket was a prostitute, Australia was broke.

Kallis looked way solider than his frame. AB looked in complete control.

Johnson produced two brilliant nuts, with a 70 over ball, then he used his pace to get rid of a nervous debutante, before two tailenders just went with the flow. People are already comparing it to the great Ambrose and McGrath spells at the WACA. Johnson didn't hit a crack in the wicket, or get help from a spicy pitch; he had a flat pitch, a settled partnership and an old ball that wasn't reversing.

This was something special, like the time I got a donkey stuffed toy out of a claw machine. Who knows if this is the making of him or not?

There still seems to be flaw in his action, but left arm bowlers who can bowl at 150 and can inspire this sort of panic are few and far between.

He is quickly becoming one of the best fast bowlers on the planet; lucky I didn't devote months to bagging him.

December 21 - Excuse me Ricky

South Africa chase down 414, second biggest chase in Test history, to win the first Test against Australia.

I don't mind losing, Ricky. Being a Victorian and a Collingwood supporter, I have a sick love for it. But losing like that, with limp dicks in your hand - that is what shits me.

There was nothing radical tried. No rabbits pulled out of anything. Not a hint of creativity. The plan seemed to revolve around giving Johnson the ball, and hoping the pitch would keep low.

No 8-1 fields, no overs of bouncers, no Krazy Krejza bowling wide of off stump, no Katich, no Symonds, and no fucking clue. You are supposed to be the captain of Australia. Not South Africa. If South Africa want to win with their defensive fields and textbook thinking, let them. That is not our way. Put a leg slip in and bowl at the hip for an over. Try Hussey with the keeper up at the stumps. Keep all the fielders up for five overs. Try something.

Because I don't mind losing to a team that does something special to win, but not one who just cruises along because you can't give them obstacles. 414 is not the score it used to be, but it's still supposed to be hard. This was not hard, they could have chased 515 just as easily. Fucken hell, if you have given up ideas give the job to someone else. Give it to the Krab, Hussey or Clarke. Bring in White or North. Hell, give it to an ageing hairless albino badger that has no eyes, no sense of direction and no hope of holding a cricket bat.

I don't care, but I refuse to go out like this. Go out playing millionaire shots. Go out with five slips three gullys and a short leg. But enough of this chicken arse shit.

December 24 - Jesus knew when to make an exit; think about it Matty

Matthew Hayden's form was one of Australia's many problems, and it was the one that seemed easiest to fix, as there were viable options in Shield cricket, and he was 83-years-old.

If you go too soon, no one will think you were dead. If you go too late, no one will care that you have gone. It's all about the timing. Jesus knew this. Matty Hayden likes to ask himself "what would Jesus do?" Sometimes that is "call India third world", and other times it's "sledge Graeme Smith".

Well Jesus would retire now, and not just because he has bad hands, but because if you stick around too long and do little, you tarnish your entire afterlife. There was a book about it once; if Hayden has time to read something that doesn't have recipes for moo shoo pork in it, he should borrow one from a hotel.

December 27 - A sizzling story

Young players stood up for both countries at the MCG.

Test cricket is a motherfucker. It is supposed to be that way. So when a young guy comes through and performs well enough to change the momentum of a Test, it's a magical fucking moment. Yesterday Peter Siddle went from hopeful to Test player.

Firstly he showed balls with the bat, and not for the first time. This was a solid as a rock innings for a number 11 against three blokes who can bowl 150 plus. This series was supposed to be about pace, Steyn had five wickets already, and the G was making the WACA look like a subbie wicket.

Siddle stood behind the ball, took one on the back, and batted for 49 balls while pissing off the South Africans. But as Tony Greig pointed out, way too many times, as good as this was, it meant nothing without wickets. Ponting obviously knew the same, and he made one of the best decisions of his career: he threw the new nut to Siddle.

Ponting hasn't been getting a lot of things right at late, and from time to time I mention that, but this was right, and he deserves the credit, unless someone else told him to do it, then they deserve it.

Who knows what was going through the kid's head at this stage, but he was on the biggest stage left in Test cricket. His home ground. New ball in hand, he fucken steamed in and swung one at pace first ball.

Second ball he almost put a hole in McKenzie's chest. It was fast and brutal. Third ball was unplayable. Fourth ball was left alone. By this stage Siddle was fire itself. He had a maniacal laugh. Pace of a demon God. And the ball was singing for him. McKenzie was no match.

It's hard to know whether he played or left the one that got him, it had pace, movement and a sexuality all of its own. Then when Smith was set he took him down, this time with no new ball help. And followed it up with one that smashed through AB's road block.

Three wickets do not make a Test player, but the boy sure looked like one.

December 28 - JP Duminy

Remember the spelling. Write it down if you have to. This was a coming out innings. This is how you greet Test cricket. It was like a Disney film about how to make your debut Test century.

His team needed it, check.
Batting with the tail when the big guns had failed, check.
Against the current number one side, check.
At the biggest cricket ground in world cricket, check.

All he needed was a girl to run out on the field as he went out, and give him a kiss as the music swelled and the camera panned around him.

The innings was created from a place of batting perfection. His footwork was genius. He was Fred Astaire with a bat, and sometimes even Ginger Rogers. His sense of moment was way beyond his years. The occasion didn't get to him, he got to it, and did the right thing at the right time.

His technique was sexy as hell. The technique was so hot you would sell your first child to Hitler if it meant your second child would have skill to bat like this.

He came out like few before him. It was Ali vs Liston. It was Zatopek in London. It was Genghis Khan in Europe. It was Lara in Sydney. It was Tendulkar, also in Sydney. Bill compared him to Neil Harvey. Nicholas compared him to Lara. Compare him to whoever you want, the boy can bat.

That was an innings that doesn't just guarantee you a career, it changes the world of cricket a little bit. Sometimes things are on your side; Steyn should have been cleaned up multiple times, and Australia was one bowler down on an increasingly flat looking wicket.

But Tendulkar and Lara didn't make their scores on tough wickets to bat on. It was how they made them that mattered.

JP made his look easy, calm and sexy, and it wasn't as if he was batting with Ravi Shastri; he had to make the runs and control the tailender at the other end. He just made the most out of every last ball.

Time will be his big test, but JP will always have this, and so will everyone who saw it.

December 29 - Bryceman

Bryce McGain had regained fitness, and was being eased back into competitive cricket. His comeback game ended up being in rural Victoria, and Cricket With Balls had the first photos publicly available of this magically wondrous occasion.

Stereotypes are hard to overcome. People see a man in his 30s, who is an IT dude, with a son and a dodgy shoulder and they think "nerd". Unfairly. The truth is way different. Cricket With Balls' Own Nice Bryce McGain is actually a crime fighter by night. It's hush hush of course, so don't tell anyone. His crime fighting name is The Prahran Panther, but don't rate him on that, he is an IT worker not a marketing executive.

While others are sleeping, he cleans the mean streets of Prahran of fuel-injected nonsense, unkempt drag queens and rogue parking inspectors. That, and not his oft-mentioned shoulder injury, is the reason for his recent hiatus. However, now the streets of Prahran are clean. This is no mean feat.

He has simply done his job, and now is ready to come back to us. Not before time, Krazy Krejza is not defensive enough and Happy Hauritz is now way too defensive. Beautiful Beau Casson is three bad months away from looking for a real job. It seems that Bryce is just right.

What Australia needs is a superhero, and since Bryce is finished on Chapel St, who better than a nerdy super spinner with wrists of gold and spectacles of hope. It makes sense.

Bryce to Sydney. And beyond.

Right now.

December 30 - And it's over

South Africa win the second Test, and beat Australia at home for the first time since 92/93.

Not just a Test, or a series, but a dynasty. And how.

Complete arse poundings in India, followed up by come from the front losses at home. The Australian cricket team will fight another day. But it will be a new team. Soon there will be no one left from the glory days. The ones who were left have been hanging onto something that did not exist.

Sri Lanka turned up first, and were despatched easily, but Kumar cut holes in her. India were handled, not always well, but the result was never really in doubt. Kumar's holes had turned into India's cracks.

No spinner. An attack that could look benign for long periods of time. A captain who realised he had no tricks. And a batting line up that was working on resumes rather than results.

The West Indies wins looked good on paper, but in real life they were working class wins born out of professionalism and little spark. Once the team got to India, it imploded, on every level. Injuries, terrible selections, family problems, incorrect administracration, and the luck of a man who has molested a leprechaun.

Then back home things looked better, a minnow was slaughtered, and confidence was restored. South Africa arrived quietly confident. Australia got to the front only to make a near record chase look like a stroll to McDonald's for Graeme Smith. They bounced back again at the G, and owned the Test match for two days, and then spent the next two days showing that they were a heavyweight boxer who leads with his right. He can make a few good hits, but he doesn't have it in him to bring the other guy down, and he has little else once the right is worked out.

The dynasty was being held together by one man who wouldn't let go, and a bunch of youngsters eager to join a club that didn't exist.

It's over now.

Time to rebuild. Let the new champions have their time in the sun. And plan for a new day.

This is the most exciting time for Australia in years: a chance for Hilfenhaus, Bollinger, Smith, Henriques, Hughes, McDonald, Geeves, Hill, Paine and Pattinson.

For the old guard things will change. The champions will get their TV gigs and book deals. The middle players will get juicy IPL contracts, jobs at sportsman's nights and invited to the odd cool party. The fringe players will pick up county and ICL contracts.

And cricket will go on.

January 7 - Graeme Smith is not a fucktard

Special bonus post, you've earned it.

Recently, when a very well respected man asked me if Graeme Smith was still a fucktard, I had to think about it. That cut me deep. I concluded that he probably still was. Then he comes out to bat with two dodgy paws (broken hand and an operated-on elbow). Hard to call him a fucktard right now.

When he was a captain of an underachieving side and he made most of his runs against the Windies, Poms and minnows, it was easy. In fact it felt great. At least in the short term he has earned some sort of rights with me.

I love players playing injured. Along with the skill to change a game in a session, captaining the side with actual thought, it is the cricket skill I most respect. I grew up with stories about Rick McCosker's jaw. It was my dad's favourite cricket story.

And the first two times I injured myself on the cricket field I refused to come off; in fact the longest I have ever been off a field with an injury was one over, to tape up my broken finger, before going back out to slip. So how can I, someone who has called his site Cricket With Balls, not respect Graeme Smith?

This is a soul-searching moment, but I have to respect him.

Of course I will still bag his defensive captaincy by numbers, and his minnow bashing, but as a cricketer, right at the moment, as I type on the keyboard and Tom Waits sings Blue Valentines, I respect Graeme Smith.

And by that I mean, he is not a fucktard.

Support your local cricket blog

well pitched - inswingers from pakistan - www.wellpitched.com

two cents - homer's odyssey - dopaisekatamasha.blogspot.com

third umpire - watch for the amber light - third-umpire.blogspot.com

the warbling willow - listen to it sing - www.thewarblingwillow.blogspot.com

the village cricketer - for village people - thevillagecricketer.wordpress.com

the tcwj - soulberry's crew - tcwj.blogspot.com

the silly point - in close - www.thesillypoint.com/blogs

the pitch report - no keys - thepitchreport.blogspot.com

the old batsman - likes it uncovered - theoldbatsman.blogspot.com

the match referee - not chris broad - blog.thematchreferee.com

the green yonder – over - www.mahendrashikaripur.com

the free hit - ankit doesn't charge - thefreehit.blogspot.com

the corridor - just outside off - www.cricket.mailliw.com

stump cam - stu's views - stumpcam.blogspot.com

straight points - from square of the wicket - straightpoints.blogspot.com

spun out - nice flight - spunout.wordpress.com

sport review - pissy kiwis - sportreview.net.nz

smart cricket talk - not silly - thegameofcricket.blogspot.com

sledgers and sandbaggers - he does both - sledgers.blogspot.com

short of a length - but does length matter? - shortofalength.wordpress.com

simply cricket - it's that - www.simplycricket.net/index.php

silly m(a)idon - no maidens here - sillymaidon.blogspot.com

side line slogger - beige is the new beige - stuff.co.nz/blogs/sidelineslogger

rousing cricket - inspiring stuff - rousingcricket.blogspot.com

reverse swing manifesto - the unablogger unloads - reverseswingmanifesto.blogspot.com

reverse sweep – gattingesque - sportwriter.wordpress.com

republique cricket - suavest cricket blog ever - republiquecricket.com

popping crease - back foot blogging - popping-crease.blogspot.com

playing accross the line - risky lady - playingacrosstheline.blogspot.com

pie chucker - serving it up - piechucker.com

pappus' plane - the stats ninja - pappubahry.blogspot.com

outside the line - appeal worthy - outsidetheline.typepad.com

outside edge - small nicks - outsideedge.wordpress.com

off the mark - virtually never dim south africans - www.offthemark.co.za

off cutter - comes in - offcutter.blogspot.com

no ballz - the women's cricket blog - no-ballz.blogspot.com

night watch girl - hoggard style - www.nightwatchgirl.com

naked cricket – nekkid - nakedcricket.blogspot.com

miss field - a warrioress - miss-field.com

mike on cricket - he is literally on cricket - mikeoncricket.blogspot.com

mid off - ottayan's position - midoff.blogspot.com

martins blog – enjoy - martinleslie.wordpress.com

maiden bowling - she keeps it tight - maidenbowling.blogspot.com

line & length - the times blog - timesonline.typepad.com/line_and_length

king cricket - bulldog grit - www.kingcricket.co.uk

just about anything - sach's slag - sachtheone.blogspot.com

island express - john's say - islandexpress.blogspot.com

iain o'brien's cricket blog - the trundler speaks - iainobrien.blogspot.com

i3j3 - indian fans - i3j3cricket.wordpress.com

history of cricket – stuart's look back - historyofcricket.blogspot.com

good areas - banh's areas - goodareas.blogspot.com

fly slip - deep cover from sri lanka - www.theflyslip.net

flintoff's ashes - drunkard or not - www.flintoffsashes.com

eye on cricket - ny's number one cricket blog -eye-on-cricket.blogspot.com

ed ladd - irish cricket diary - edladd.blogspot.com

drinks break - his shout - drinksbreak.blogspot.com

doosra - the other one - gonewiththewindies.blogspot.com

different shades of green - lovely colours - differentshadesofgreen.blogspot.com

crucket - ben gets vowel - crucket.co.nz

cricville - visit it now - cricville.blogspot.com

cricketua - take a look at cricket - www.cricketua.com

crickosphere - round coverage - onlycricketplease.blogspot.com

cricket3r - 3asy cricket feeds - cricket3r.com

cricket, a brilliant game! - exclamation! - whoplayscricket.blogspot.com

cricket za - not that evil - cricketza.com

cricket statistics - numbers n such - cricketstatistics.in

cricket rules – ok - www.cricket-rules.com

cricket plus news – indeed - cricketplusnews.blogspot.com

cricket n all that - a guru speaks - cricketandallthat.blogspot.com

cricket keeper - he is behind you - cricketkeeper.blogspot.com

cricket god - strangely it's not about me - www.cricketgod.com

cricket funs - showbag goodies - cricket-funs.blogspot.com

cricket forever - a long time - cricket-forever.blogspot.com

cricket fizz – isaac's law - www.cricketfizz.com/cricketblog

cricket files - discover the x - cricketfiles.com

cricket fever - it's live cricket - cricketfever.org

cricket fans - Icl news and views - www.cricket247.in

cricket fanatic – fantastic - www.cricketfanatic.com

cricket etc - it's written by a 12 year old girl they tell me - crick3tetc.blogspot.com

cricket buzz - it buzzes - www.cricketbuzz.org

cricket blog - Jc's spin - www.cricket-blog.com

cricket ahead - not behind - cricketahead.blogspot.com

cricket action art - pretty pictures - www.cricketactionart.blogspot.com

cricket 24 x 7 - some indian flavour - www.cricket24x7.blogspot.com

cow corner - cricket agriculture - geethakrishnan.blogspot.com

cover points - dream position - community.dreamcricket.com/community/blogs/cover_points

chinese cuts - not french - highyengar.wordpress.com

charlie randall - not steve - www.charlierandall.org

caribbean cricket - windie news - caribbeancricket.com/weblog

canary yellow - bill's favourite colour - canaryyellowblog.blogspot.com

buzz in cricket - hum dinger - www.buzzincricket.co.uk

breathing cricket – deep - breathingcricket.blogspot.com

bored cricket crazy indians - is there another kind - http://boredcricketcrazyindians.blogspot.com

bouncy & curvy - like kate winslet jogging - www.bouncyandcurvy.blogspot.com

beige brigade - they wear it and live it - www.beigebrigade.co.nz/blog

beer & sport - on tap - www.beerandsport.net

arm ball - around the wicket - armball.blogspot.com

are you a left arm chinaman - well are you? - leftarmchinaman.blogspot.com

all padded up - kitted and ready to go - www.allpaddedup.com

after grog blog - a cricket blog occasionally - aftergrogblog.blogs.com

99.94 - above average - nestaquin.wordpress.com

4th umpire - not a bad gig - 4thumpire.blogspot.com

4.5 inches of wood - that's all you'll need - 4point5inches.blogspot.com

Huge thank you to everyone on this list.

Mum & Dad, none of this would have happened without your love, piss taking, support, and belief in me. Sorry I dropped out of Gardening school and didn't join the army.

Miriam, I don't know what I would do without you, I must thank Rahul Dravid someday.

Joel, Todd & Simon, every conversation we had was a warm up, you are the brothers I never had.

Isabella, for being the beautiful reason they called me Uncle.

Blair, for the angry cricket with the big balls.

The Kimbers & Marshalls, thank you for everything.

Sarge, you're a pretty good bloke for someone who lives in New Texas, I owe you one.

Bonga Bonga & Mrs Bonga Bonga, for treating me like I was someone.

Alex Picahci, I can never thank you enough for believing in me.

The Ahamats, Sariman, and Kilbys for treating me as one of their own.

Ed Craig, for changing my life.

Gideon, for the foreword, the support and lending the book some legitimacy.

Miss Field, for being Miss Field and helping with the book.

Jeremy, for the cover.

Dibyo, for the cricket with balls prototype cricketer.

Campbellfield Cricket Club, where I learnt the game.

Kicker & Tony, sitting at your feet I learnt about cricket & life.

Coburg Cricket Club, thank you gentleman, and you too Tucky.

Johnny & Bender, for letting me go, and the many drunken late night chats.

Kev, Jason & Mumbles, apparently all that time in the nets wasn't wasted.

Adriana, see I told you bad grammar would never hold me back.

Sarah, one day I'll read your book.

Bryce McGain, for not thinking I was a stalker, and providing hope.

Dirk Nannes & Natalie Portman, for inspiration.

Sehwag, for the spiritual guidance.

©hinaman for the website maintenance, design and help.

Graeme, for the yoda like advice.

Suave, for the invention of the word fucktard, and being a top bloke.

Andrew Mosey, for the help and aussieness.

Umair, for the excitement and Pakistani view.

Soulberry, for being my first real commenter, and talking me up as a writer.

Ceci, Sarah & Mel for the help with photos and the fanatic behaviour.

Johnny, for mentioning the book idea, you're a token aussie now.

King Cricket, for showing us how it's done.

All the cricket bloggers for their work.

The cricketers, thanks for the inspiring and uninspiring deeds.

The commenters on the site, you keep me ranting on.

The silent visitors on the site, thanks for stopping by.

And a special thank you to Ms Hooper, you said I was too stupid to write anything good, you might still be right, but stick this book up your ass just the same.

Books made from cricket blogs were better in my day – NH

Printed in Great Britain
by Amazon.co.uk, Ltd.,
Marston Gate.